'For my Mother'
F. G.

© for the French edition: Saltimbanque Éditions, 2018
25 bd Romain Rolland · 75 014 Paris
Title of the Original edition: *Curieuse Nature*
© for the English edition: Prestel Verlag, Munich · London · New York, 2018
A member of Verlagsgruppe Random House GmbH
Neumarkter Strasse 28 · 81673 Munich

Prestel Publishing Ltd.
14-17 Wells Street
London W1T 3PD

Prestel Publishing
900 Broadway, Suite 603
New York, NY 10003

Library of Congress Control Number: 2017964037
A CIP catalogue record for this book is available from the British Library.

Translated from the French by Paul Kelly

Copyediting: Brad Finger
Project management: Melanie Schöni
Production management: Astrid Wedemeyer
Typesetting: textum GmbH
Paper: Gardamat Ultra

MIX
Paper from
responsible sources
FSC® C014075

Verlagsgruppe Random House FSC® N001967

Printed in Italy

ISBN 978-3-7913-7365-2
www.prestel.com

Florence Guiraud

Wonders of Nature

Explorations in the World of Birds, Insects and Fish

Prestel

Munich · London · New York

Preface

At the time of the Enlightenment, during the 17th and 18th centuries, European kings and queens funded missions to explore continents around the world. These remarkable journeys were inspired by both curiosity and the desire for riches. Among the explorers who took part were scientists and artists – people who could describe and draw the fascinating plants and animals they encountered in these far away places. With a keen eye for detail, these artist explorers produced extraordinary picture boards and sketchbooks. I have always been fascinated by their images, which used to feed my imagination and, in some cases, remained in my memory for a very long time. Sketches, watercolors, engravings – their pictures were made as scientific records, yet they are also seen today as works of art. As close to reality as the artists could make them, the images have great beauty, sometimes simple and often overwhelming. My wish with this book was to arrange the pictures in subjects that fascinated me the most, something like a cabinet of curiosities.

When it comes to nature, each of us has our own interests and sensibilities. Some prefer to observe, others need to touch, while still others want to listen. Above all, though, it's the beauty of nature that imposes itself on us. I invite you into my cabinet of natural poetry…

Florence Guiraud

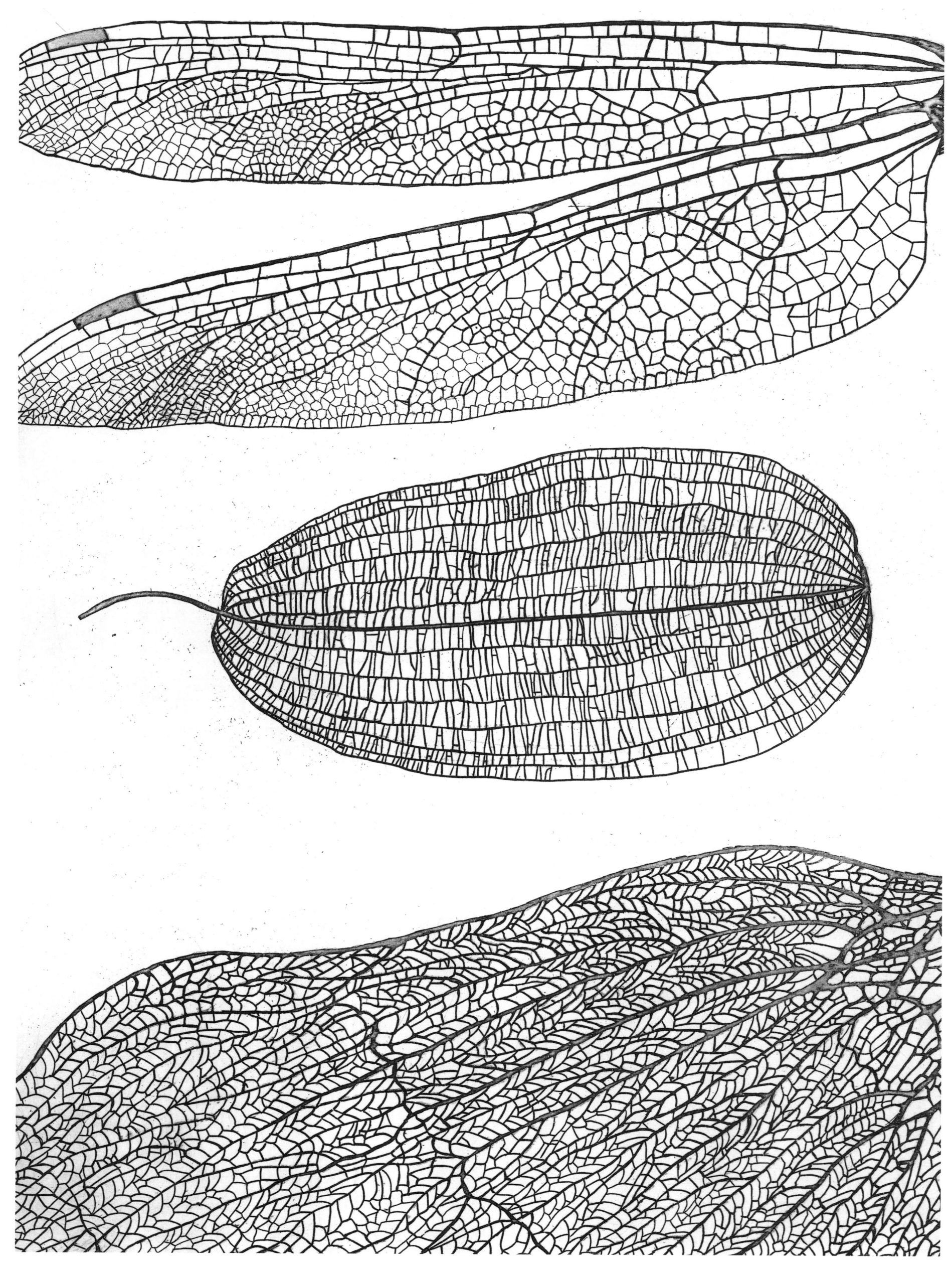

Content

7/20   "Les Oiseaux"   F. Guigui

01

Birds through a magnifying glass

The genius of nature

There are nearly 10,000 species of birds around the world, and we continue to discover more every year. From the largest to the smallest, birds are marvels of nature; they have colonized the skies, the earth and the oceans. The planet is theirs. They can be spotted during any season of the year. They are everywhere and all around us. We recognize their silhouettes. I discovered big ones, tiny ones, black ones, multi-colored ones, funny ones and scary ones, too. Just look at the great potoo, with its huge, bulging, yellow eyes. Birds have different temperaments. Some are chatty, others quiet, and still others love to make music – just like the nightingale's song of love. I counted more than one hundred verbs used to describe the birdsong. Birds have many talents; some cross the continents, whilst others have no clue about flying. Not knowing how to fly is astonishing for a bird! The kiwi, for example, spends its entire life on the ground without a care for being up in the air. Its wings have wasted away over time, whilst its legs have grown larger and more muscular. Now it just runs about on the ground. Nature finds a way to adapt.

Whatever their size, all birds lay eggs, have two wings and two legs, are covered in feathers and have beaks bereft of teeth. Some can be dangerous, such as the cassowary with its large foot claw. Other birds can be tender and affectionate. In my research, I discovered all manner of bird occupations: from incredible dancers, surprising and unexpected singers, fabulous acrobats, right through to the satin bowerbird that decorates its nest with all kinds of blue objects. Birds are truly eye-catching. How could one fail to notice the captivating look of nocturnal owls, the finesse of the rock ptarmigan's fluffy down feathers or the lavish coloring of the harlequin duck's plumage? And certainly, you've noticed the delicate long necks of swans or other wading birds, an absolute picture of pure grace. These extraordinary creatures continue to amaze us!

Victoria Crowned Pigeon

Palm Cockatoo

Southern Rockhopper Penguin

Lyrebird

Livingstone's Turaco

Royal Spoonbill

Grey Crowned Crane

Turquoise-Browed Motmot

Royal Flycatcher

Tufted Coquette

Peacock

Snowy Egret

Shoebill

Mandarin Duck

Madagascan Ibis

Hoatzin

Yellow-Billed Stork

Helmet Vanga

Asian Openbill

Marabou Stork

Shoebill

Raven

Pelican

Scarlet Ibis

Kiwi

Reed Cormorant

Trumpeter Hornbill

Northern Shoveler

Lovebird

Great Blue Heron

Spoonbill

Kea

Lappet-Faced Vulture

Avocet

Sword-Billed Hummingbird

Toco Toucan

Griffon Vulture

Northern Fulmar

Hamerkop

Quelea

Eurasian Blue Tit

Flamingo

Northern Gannet

Ostrich

Puffin

Eurasian Eagle-Owl

Saddle-Billed Stork

Barn Owl

Hooded Merganser

European Green Woodpecker

King Vulture

Duck

Reddish Egret

Blue Crane

Grey Heron

Flamingo

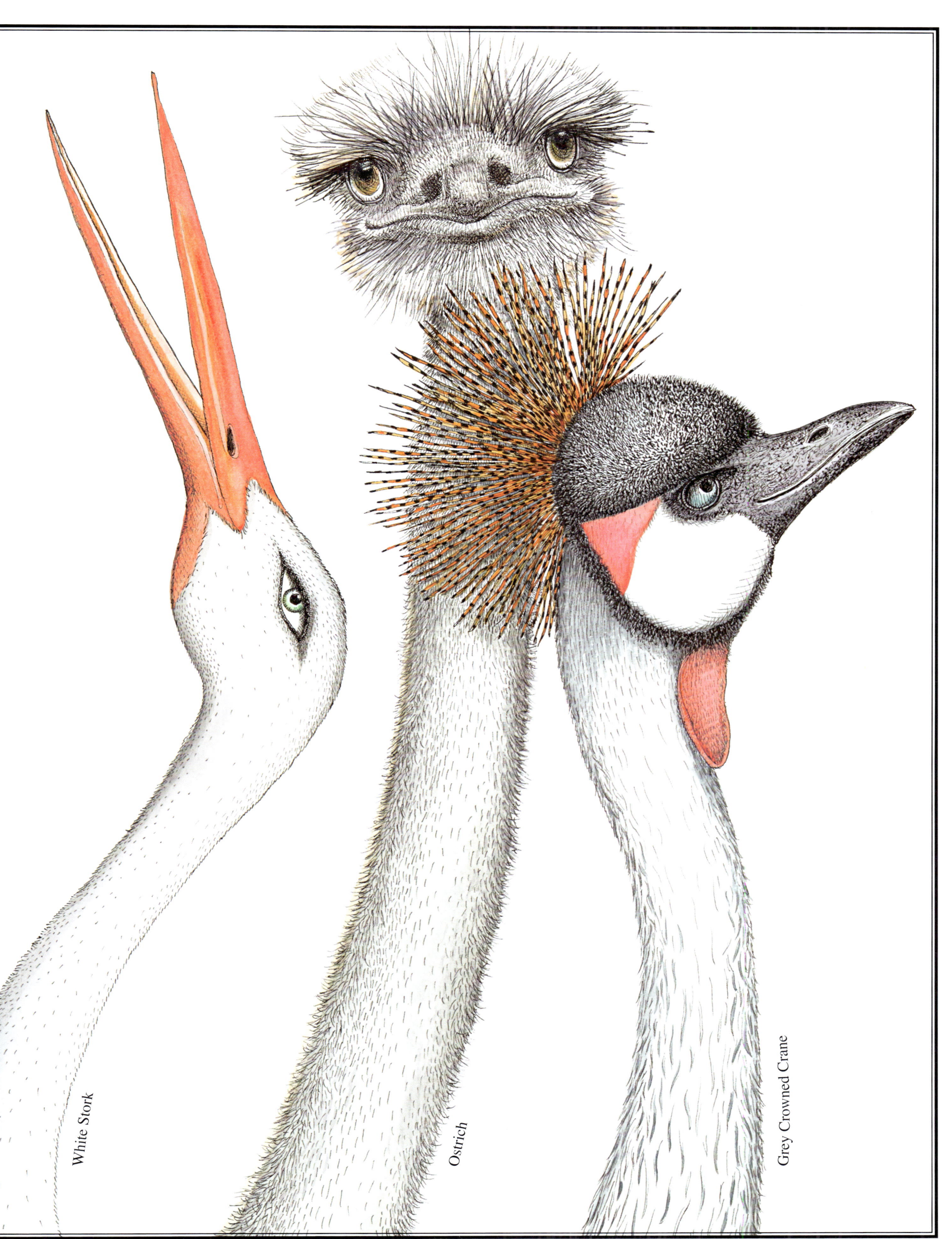

White Stork

Ostrich

Grey Crowned Crane

Blue Jay

Ostrich

Royal Flycatcher

Southern Masked Weaver

Tailorbird

Eurasian Reed Warbler

White Stork

Flamingo

Grizzly Rooster

Vulturine Guineafowl

Rooster

Golden Pheasant

Wilson's Bird-of-Paradise

Common Pheasant

Northern Cardinal

Eurasian Jay

Great Argus

Tragopan

Superb Lyrebird

Eurasian Magpie

European Herring Gull

European Golden Plover

Swan

Mallard

Ostrich

Griffon Vulture

Buzzard

Silver Pheasant

Grey Heron

Long-Tailed Tit

Budgerigar

Malayan Peacock-Pheasant

Mandarin Duck

Cuckoo

Lady Amherst's Pheasant

Wood Warbler

Quetzal

Western Crowned Pigeon

Blue Eared Pheasant

Common Blackbird

Starling

Dromaius

Eurasian Oystercatcher

Peacock

Cockatoo

Montezuma Oropendola

Eagle

Owl

Guillemot

Great Spotted Woodpecker

Eurasian Penduline Tit

Baltimore Oriole

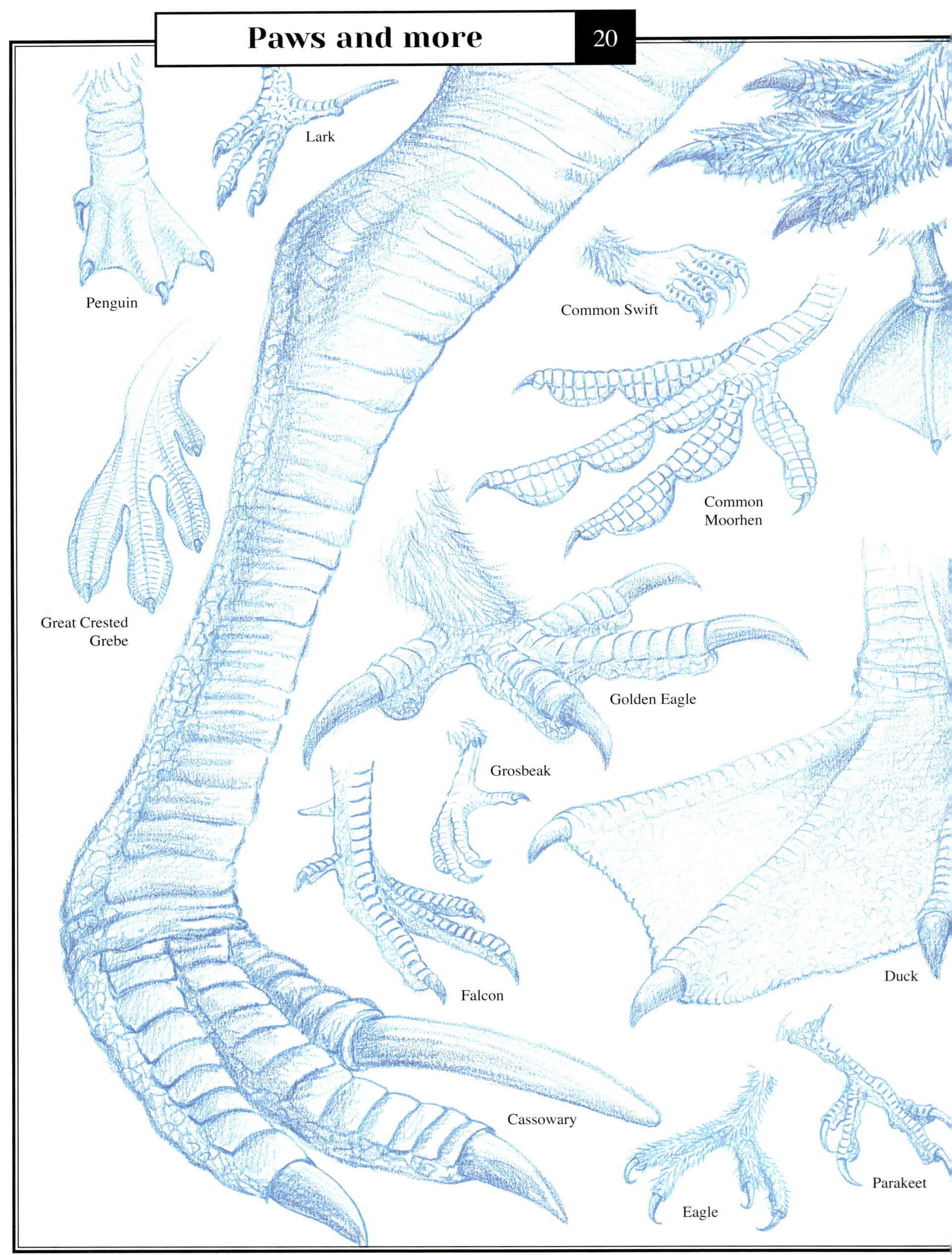

Penguin

Lark

Common Swift

Great Crested
Grebe

Common
Moorhen

Golden Eagle

Grosbeak

Falcon

Duck

Cassowary

Eagle

Parakeet

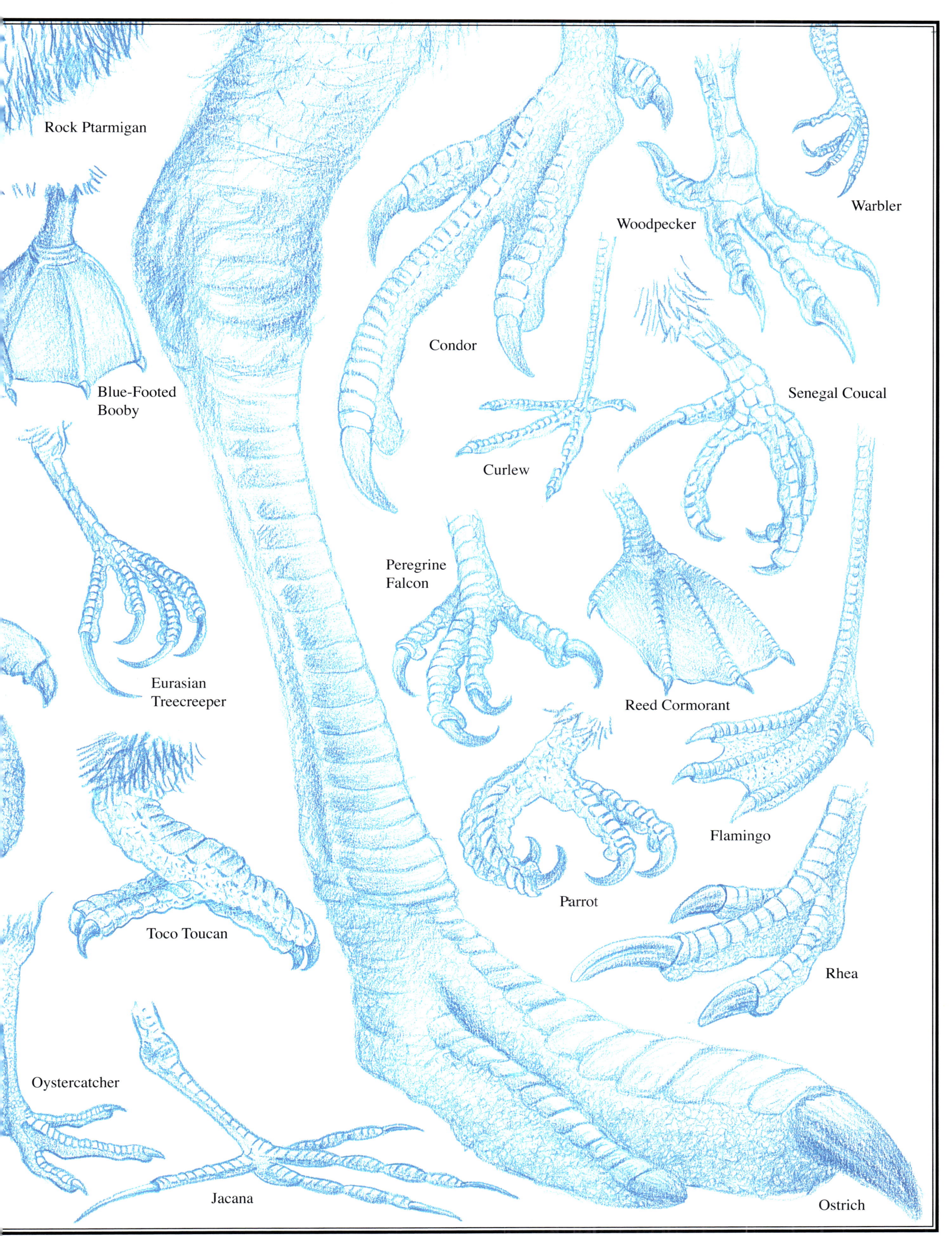

Rock Ptarmigan

Blue-Footed
Booby

Eurasian
Treecreeper

Toco Toucan

Oystercatcher

Jacana

Condor

Curlew

Peregrine
Falcon

Woodpecker

Warbler

Senegal Coucal

Reed Cormorant

Parrot

Flamingo

Rhea

Ostrich

Barred Eagle-Owl

Barn Owl

Black-and-White Owl

Tawny Owl

Oriental Bay Owl

Snowy Owl

Great Horned Owl

Great Grey Owl

Random Directory

Albatross
This bird can reach the grand old age of 60 years – a veritable old-timer. But at 3 years old, its offspring are already quite mature.

Shoebill
This rare bird is tall and solid, but it's the huge head and massive bill that gets all the attention. (13;14)

Penguin
This bird is a veritable submarine, capable of diving up to 400 meters (1,312 feet) underwater. (20)

Cockatoo
What better way to cool off than to take a nice shower? Cockatoos know this all too well – they hang upside down, spreading their big wings in the rain. (12;19)

Arctic Tern
This bird would certainly rack up frequent flyer miles on any airline! It flies about 71,000 kilometers (44,000 miles) round trip during its annual journey between Greenland and the Arctic – a total of 8 months in the air.

Wrinkled Hornbill
The protuberance on this bird's bill is amazing. Thankfully, this helmet-like structure (or casque) is hollow and lightweight. It even comes in handy as a sounding board when the bird screeches.

Jacana
Using its extremely long feet and claws, this bird can skip and balance on broad aquatic plant leaves without sinking in the water. (21)

Puffin
When moving underwater, this bird shakes its wings and not its webbed feet. (14/15)

Cassowary
Watch out for this bird! Its sharp, 12 centimeter (4.7 inch) talons can be used to strike animals and even people that threaten it. (20)

Rock Ptarmigan
Snowshoes to get about in the snow? They could have been designed by this Arctic bird. With feathers on its paws, it's no problem for the rock ptarmigan to walk over snow. (20/21)

Tawny Owl
Its hearing is so sharp that it can tell when a vole is running into its burrow, even as raindrops land on the leaves above it! (22)

Inca Tern
Does your cat have a moustache? This bird has one as well! At the base of its beak, the fine "moustache" feathers are used to guide the bird at night – as well as help it sniff out food.

Royal Flycatcher
To scare away predators, this tiny bird spreads out its large, pretty red crest like a fan. It's a beautiful sight! (13;18)

Kiwi
A kiwi's wing is ridiculously short, but that's okay. It cannot fly, anyway. (14)

Swiftlet
Wouldn't it be strange to eat a bird's nest? Some people still spend a fortune just to sample 'Swallow's Nest Soup'. This white nest belongs to the swiftlet of Indonesia, which is a cousin of the swallow. Made from the bird's saliva, the nest is entirely edible and said to have medicinal uses – at least that's what people say!

Hummingbird
Champion of all the flyers in the sky, this bird can even fly in reverse! (14/15)

White-Throated Dipper
The ultimate diving bird, it has powerful wings and can swim and walk on riverbeds

Royal Albatross
With all its wings outstretched, this superhero of the sky can fly through the air with a stunning wingspan of 3.7 meters (12.1 feet)!

Lyrebird
When you hear the barking of a dog, the rustling of the wind and the racket of a chainsaw, then you can bet it's the lyrebird. This animal is gifted with the amazing ability to imitate sounds! (12)

Swan
Patience is needed when counting this bird's feathers. There are usually about 20,000 of them! (18)

Peregrine Falcon
This hunter can dive in the air faster than any other animal. But because of its speed, it often misses its prey. (21)

Ostrich
The male ostrich has several mates, and all of his 'lady' ostriches lay their eggs in the same nest. But only the male's favorite gets to inhabit the nest. (15;17;18/19;21)

Tailorbird
Nest building is a remarkable craft for the tailorbird! This little warbler picks out two very beautiful leaves and then threads through some cobweb silk or liana fibers to make its nest. (18)

Australian Pelican
This fellow has the longest beak of all birds, measuring in at 47 centimeters (18.5 inches).

Bearded Vulture
This one loves bone marrow. But to break the biggest of bones, he has to drop them in full flight so that they crash on jagged rocks or other hard objects.

Black Swift
This insatiable traveler is capable of staying in the air for more than eight months without landing.

Asian Openbill
You know this bird is crazy about snails because of the way nature has made its beak bent and pincer-like – perfect for capturing a meal! (14)

Flamingo
This bird has a strange way of standing. It puts one of its long legs under its wing and then performs a balancing act with the other! (15;16;18;21)

Blue Jay
Like most birds, this one does not need its nest for sleeping. As long as it finds a branch or a twig that it can hold onto tightly, it falls asleep. The nest is for its eggs and chicks. (18)

Harlequin Duck
'Give my name to a duck', said the harlequin clown, 'and that might hurt me. Yet it is so beautiful, I am, therefore, honored'.

Peacock
Even though the peacock has such beautiful plumage, it also has one of the most frightful and discordant cries in the entire bird family. It is said that the peacock bellows! (12/13;19)

Spoonbill
When wading, this bird creates a great arc on the water's surface. Then, with its huge spatula-shaped beak, it captures all the fish it needs to eat. (14)

Mallard
Whenever this duck falls asleep, it regularly pops open its eyes while still sleeping to check for predators. (18)

4/15   Poules .

02

Hens, turkeys, pheasants and the like

From dinosaurs to galliforms – it's just a small footstep in the history of evolution!

Researchers go even further than that by claiming that our harmless hens, like all birds, are cousins of the horrible *Tyrannosaurus rex*. A more recent revelation by paleontologists (people who study ancient life) discovered through several fossils that some dinosaurs had feathers.

There are many other similarities, especially in the skeletal formation of birds, that have also supported the notion that birds and dinosaurs are closely related. All of this is quite surprising to me! But then again, that's the curiosity of nature.

These big land birds, with their magnetic charm and elegant, colorful plumage, have been depicted by artists in a way worthy of the Great Masters of painting. Artists have been interested in galliforms and the like since the dawn of time. *Acryllium vulturinum*, better known as the vulturine guineafowl of Africa, was even illustrated in ancient Egyptian hieroglyphics.

I discovered the ocellated turkey, an incredible animal that, with funny orange balls around its eyes and on its beak, could well hail from a Brazilian carnival. And there is the tragopan, a spotted pheasant with blue horns and a turquoise and red bib! This bird's magnificent plumage adorned the hats of grand ladies during the last century. In spite of all the feathers, tragopans have trouble flying. They'll make a few flaps of their wings to get on a tree branch or pass the night away, but otherwise, do not expect more. These are land birds. Galliforms were the first bird types to be domesticated by humans: 6,000 BC to be exact. Since then, they have become part of our daily life. The rooster alone symbolizes so many things, from the start of day to bravery, virility and, of course, singing. In truth, however, the rooster shows himself at daybreak to look for hens and to chase away his rivals.

Hamburg Chicken

Leghorn Chicken

Houdan Chicken

Java Chicken

Pavilly Chicken

Silkie Chicken

La Flèche Chicken

Padovana Chicken

Helmeted Guineafowl

Bulwer's Pheasant

Vulturine Guineafowl

Siamese Fireback Pheasant

Blue Eared Hokki

Lady Amherst's Pheasant

Golden Gallic Rooster

Ocellated Turkey

Wild Turkey

Pucheran Crested Guineafowl

Golden Pheasant

Random Directory

Indonesian Black Hen
Can you imagine New Zealand's All Blacks rugby football team in a chicken run? Well, you might see something similar with this Indonesian poultry type. Everything about the bird is black, inside and out: its feathers, beak, feet and bones. Even its flesh is black. However, owning an Indonesian black hen comes at a high price. One bird can cost more than £1,275 ($1,800)! (32)

Silkie Chicken
This little chicken is very amiable, and when stroked its feathers feel like a cat's fur: soft and silky. Some people even keep the bird as a house pet. (29)

Java Chicken
With its strange crest, the Java chicken looks like it has a doormat on its head! This large crest is very fragile, however, and if it's not protected, the Java chicken can get frostbite in winter. (28)

Padovana Chicken
This hen is without a crest. Instead, its head is completely covered by an amazing tuft of feathers fit for a queen! Indeed, Queen Marie Antoinette of France actually kept these birds in the henhouse at the Petit Trianon palace in Versailles… (29)

Leghorn Chicken
If the preference is for extremely white eggs, as it is with Americans, then this is the bird of choice. The Leghorn is an excellent laying bird with eggs of an immaculate white hue. (28)

La Flèche Chicken
Instead of a crest, this very old breed of chicken has two small, red horns. It's why we've long called it the 'Devil Hen'. (29)

Houdan Chicken
This used to be the chicken of royalty. With its meat particularly prized, it was cooked and served at the courts of Versailles, St. Petersburg and London. Nowadays, it has become very rare. (28)

Hamburg Chicken
This bird's crest is said to be 'pearled'. The Hamburg has no perspiration system, so its crest is there to keep the bird's body temperature from getting too hot. (28)

Pavilly Chicken
Just because a hen can lay eggs, it doesn't always mean she will help them hatch. The Pavilly hen is a good egg layer, but not to be trusted when it comes to incubating. (29)

Golden Gallic Rooster
In French culinary tradition, the crests of roosters are part of many recipes. Yet, this ingredient is hard to find at any market stall today. (31)

Helmeted or Namibian Guineafowl
This African fowl, like its cousins, has one major drawback: it screeches. The bird can smash eardrums with its almost incessant cry. It's all very unpleasant!

Vulturine Guineafowl
With its huge beak, plumed neck and almost bald head, this bird resembles a vulture. Hence the name! (18;30)

Bulwer's Pheasant
This magnificent pheasant from the island of Borneo in Southeast Asia is covered in huge feathers. It almost looks like it's wearing a frilly dancer's costume from the Folies-Bergère, a famous cabaret theater in Paris. Sadly, though, the Bulwer's is classified as under threat because of poachers and deforestation. (30)

Golden Pheasant

As a form of bait, anglers use the feathers of this beautiful pheasant to imitate or replace the 'fly' at the end of their lines. (18;31)

Pucheran Crested Guineafowl

In the beginning, all guinea fowl came from Africa. When African slaves were transported to the New World, these birds went the same way. It's even said that they became a symbol of freedom when the slaves rebelled against their so-called 'masters'. The Pucheran variety is quite amusing in that it has a curly puff on its head. (31)

Wild Turkey

To avoid its predators, this turkey actually sleeps in trees. Getting airborne and climbing branches is quite a feat for a bird of this type. (31)

Ocellated Turkey

During the mating season, little orange balls appear on the male's head to make him become brighter and more prominent. This season is a bad time to irritate the bird, as it might just jab you with its 4 centimeter (1.5 inch) long spurs. (31)

Siamese Fireback Pheasant

The head of this unique pheasant is almost completely covered by a bright red skin growth, which swells up when it is trying to attract a mate. (30)

Blue-Eared Hokki

This beautiful bird almost became extinct. Its feathers were once highly prized to adorn the hats of Mandarin Chinese dignitaries. Later, during the Belle Époque era (1871-1914), the feathers appeared on hats made for wealthy ladies in Europe and other parts of the world. Fortunately, the massive exploitation of these wild birds became regulated. It needed to! It got to the stage that not just the head but even the whole bird was being used in making elegant headdresses. (30)

Lady Amherst's Pheasant

This beautiful bird is a veritable array of colors! In its native China, it is called the 'Diamond Pheasant'. (19;30)

The Egg

During the first years of its life, a chicken lays an average of 300 eggs a year. And contrary to what is believed, the shell's coloration does not depend on what the bird eats, but on its breed.

The Chick

Chicks are very garrulous. Even whilst still shut in their shells, they can be heard squeaking before they hatch.

The Eyes

The eyes of hens are quite independent of each other. One can be watching you, while the other is checking on her chicks.

The Crests

When a rooster's or chicken's crest stands upright and gets redder, there is only one reason. It's a sign of great danger.

The Crest of the Rooster

Hyaluronic acid might be known as an ingredient in many anti-wrinkle creams. What is little known, though, is that it can be extracted from rooster crests.

03

Insects of all types

Get out the microscope and check out these insects!

This tête-à-tête might surprise you, or even scare you. Don't their bizarre shapes make them look like Martians? It's hardly surprising that so many artists feel inspired by this insect universe and believe that such creatures must have come from another world. Specialists discover new insect types year in and year out. It is difficult to put a figure on the number of species inhabiting our planet. Some say a million, others reckon more. One thing is for sure: in the animal world, insects are the most numerous. They are to be found everywhere on earth: from icy regions to burning deserts, indoors and outdoors, upstairs and downstairs and in the air around us. Insects simply adapt to all climates and to the harshest conditions. Harmful, nasty, dangerous, etc… Everyone attributes destructiveness to insects! Yet, their presence can also be beneficial to people. This fact was known as far back as the age of the pharaohs in ancient Egypt. Crickets, maggots, ants, beetles… our ancestors knew of the virtues of these little beasties! Today, as many people are seeking natural forms of medicine, some are rediscovering old ways of using insects to care for themselves. In one example, which comes from China, cockroaches can be transformed into a type of antibiotic. Whether they are flying, crawling or toddling along, all insects play a role in the balance of our ecosystem. They are like gardeners, ensuring the pollination of a whole host of plant life. About 35 % of what we eat depends on such insects. And where would the Chinese textile industry be without the mulberry silkworm, a creature capable of releasing a single silk thread up to 1.5 kilometers (0.9 mile) in length. The insect world still needs to be discovered, and its potential remains largely untapped. It is time we protected them because, who knows, they may be the ones to protect us in the future.

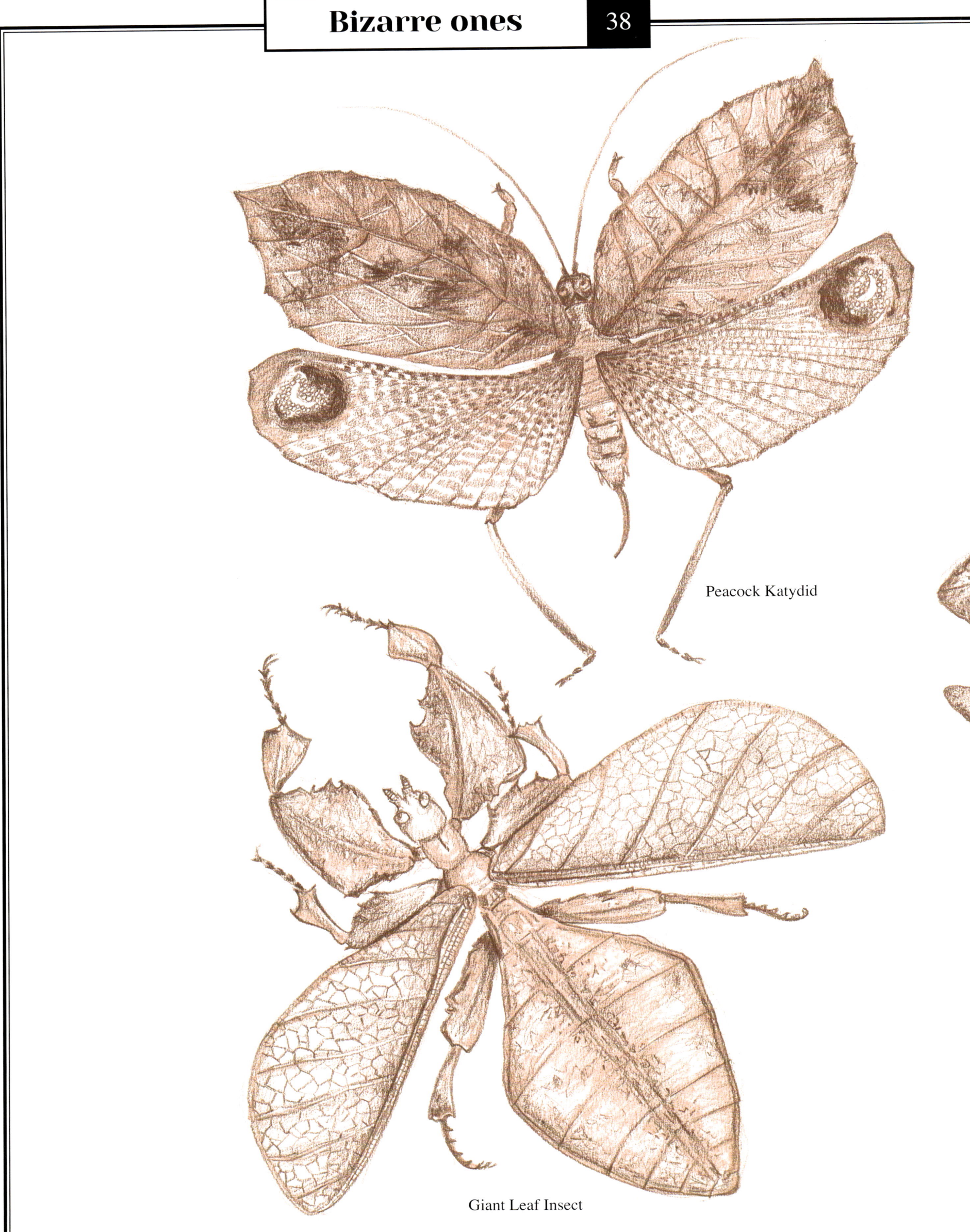

Peacock Katydid

Giant Leaf Insect

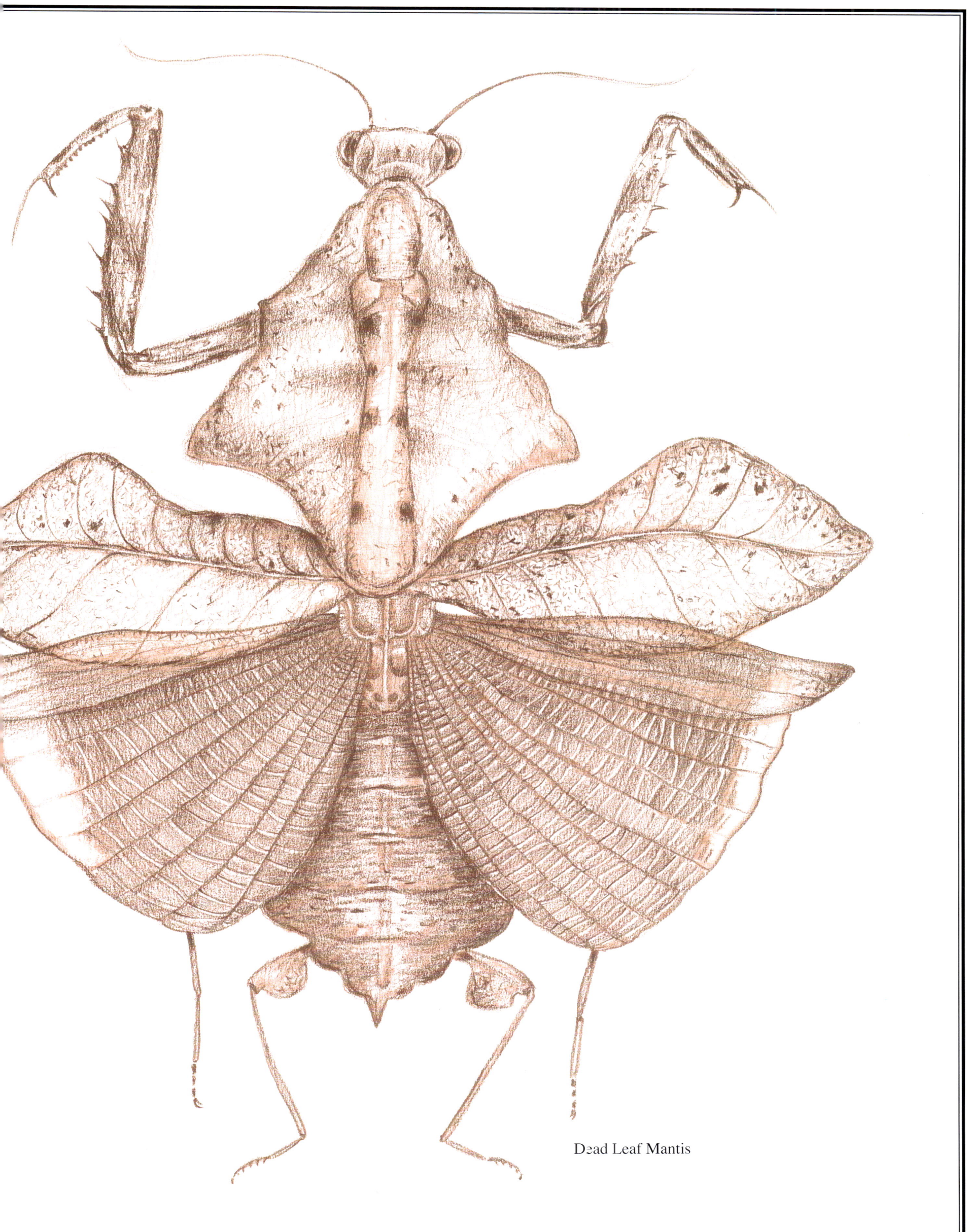

Dead Leaf Mantis

Umbonia spinosa

Exotic Charançon

Red Cabbage Shield Bug

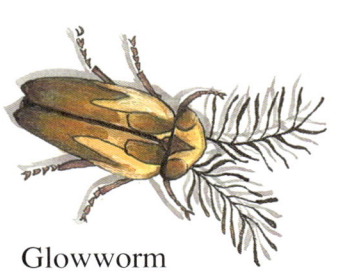

Glowworm

Beehive Beetle

Birch Bug

Spiny Tachnid Fly

Tiger Cactus Bug

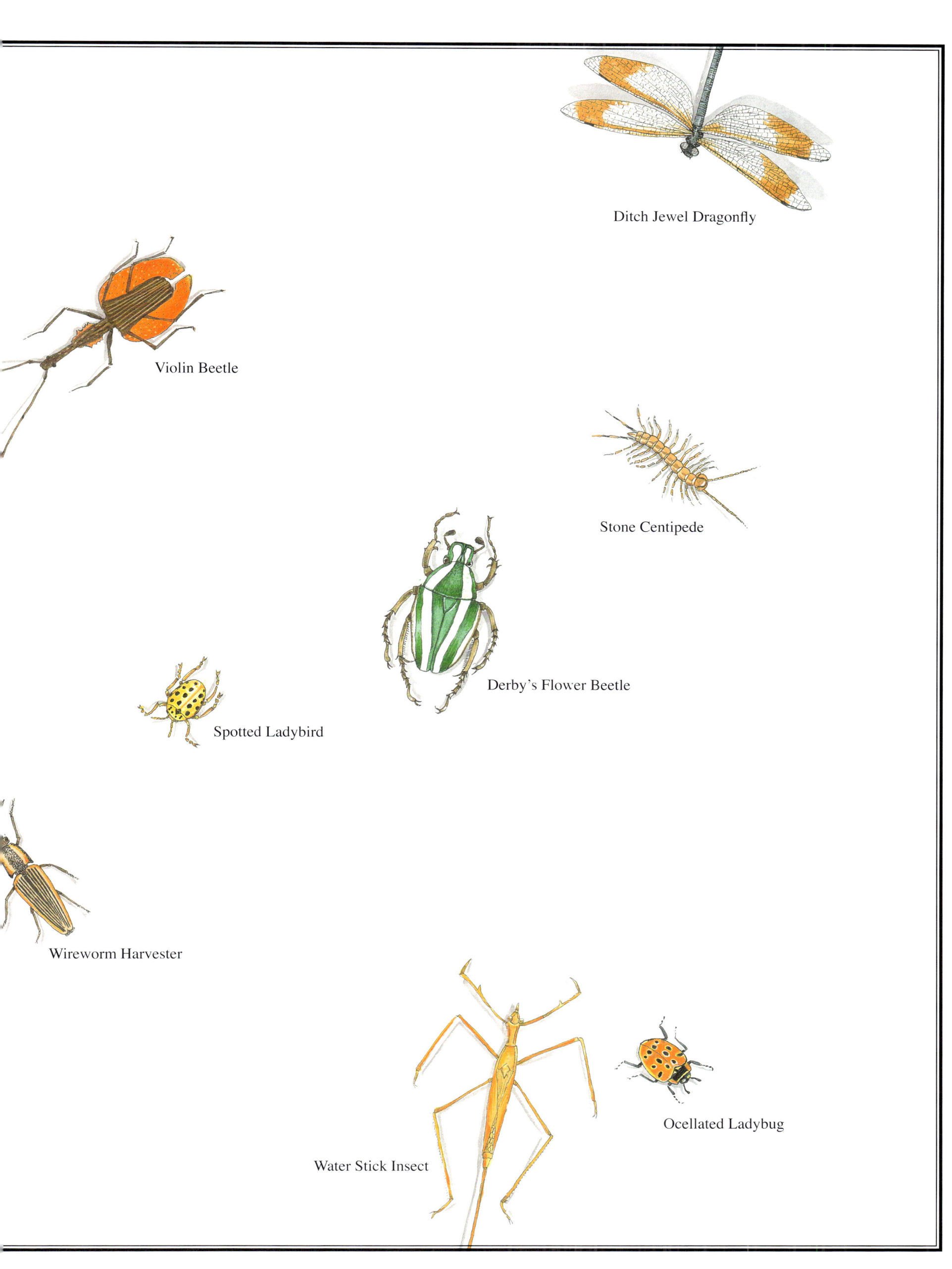

Ditch Jewel Dragonfly

Violin Beetle

Stone Centipede

Derby's Flower Beetle

Spotted Ladybird

Wireworm Harvester

Water Stick Insect

Ocellated Ladybug

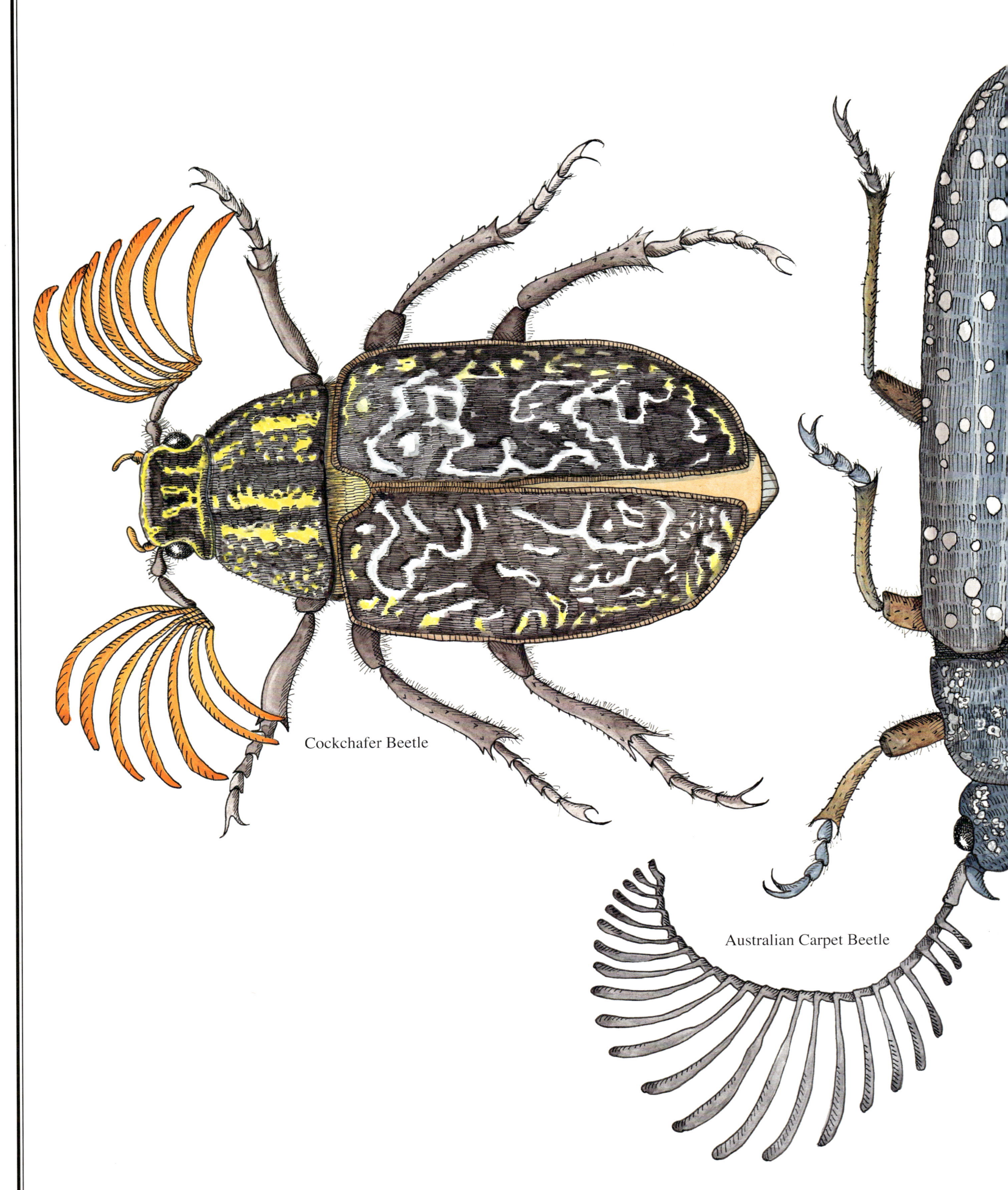

Cockchafer Beetle

Australian Carpet Beetle

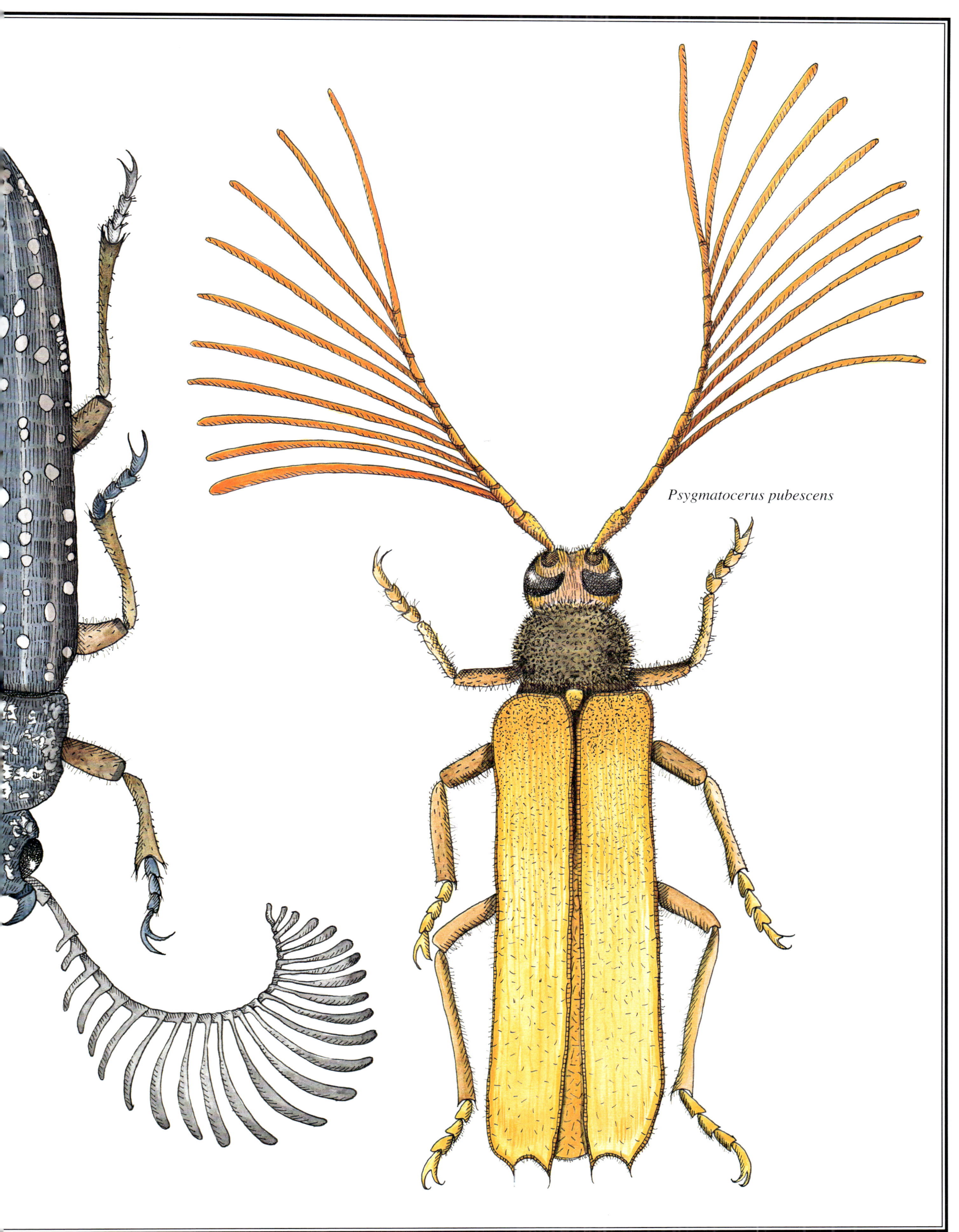

Psygmatocerus pubescens

Elegant dragonflies 44

Emperor Dragonfly
Banded Demoiselle
Guldsmed Dragonfly
Four-Spotted Chaser
Yellow-Winged Darter

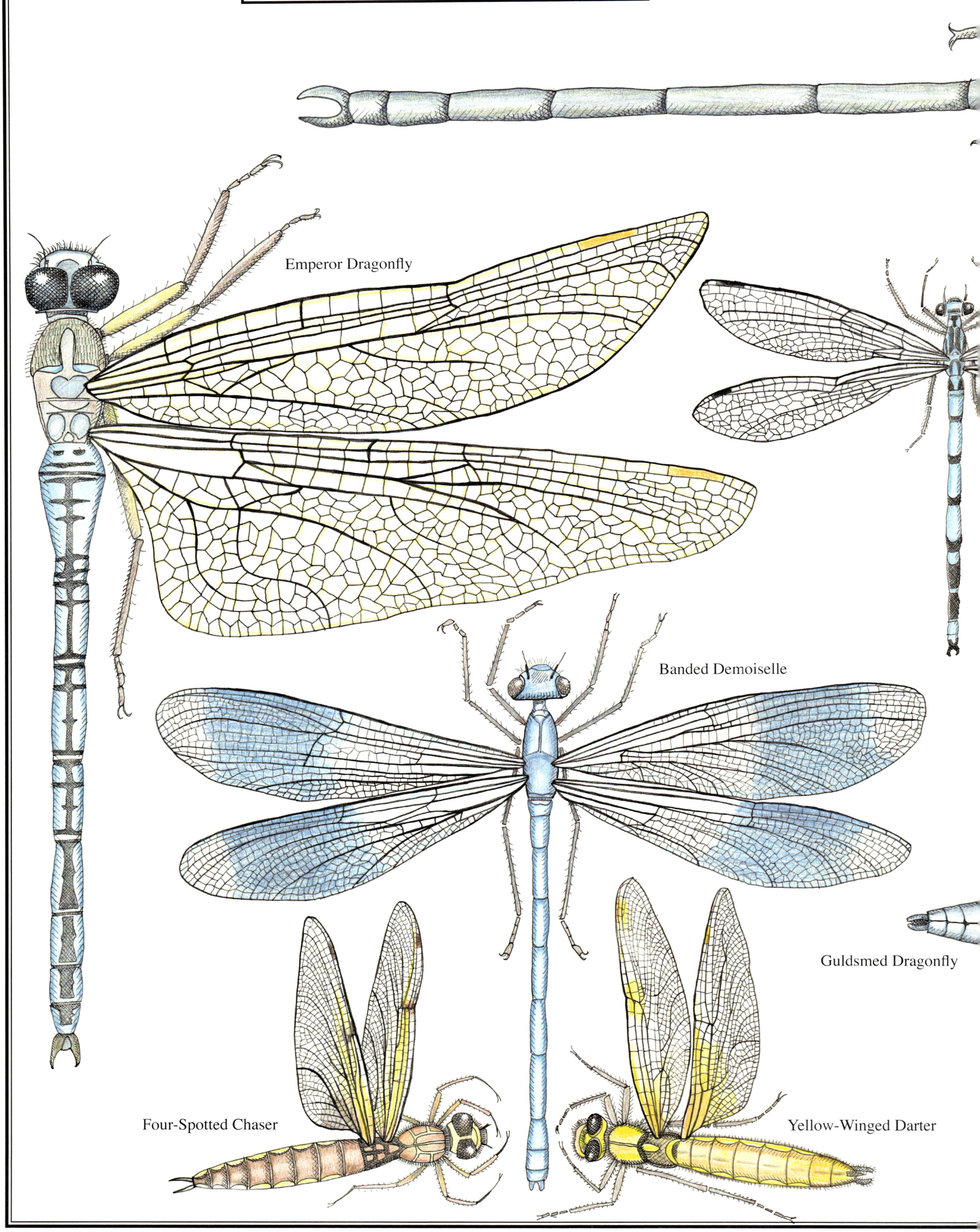

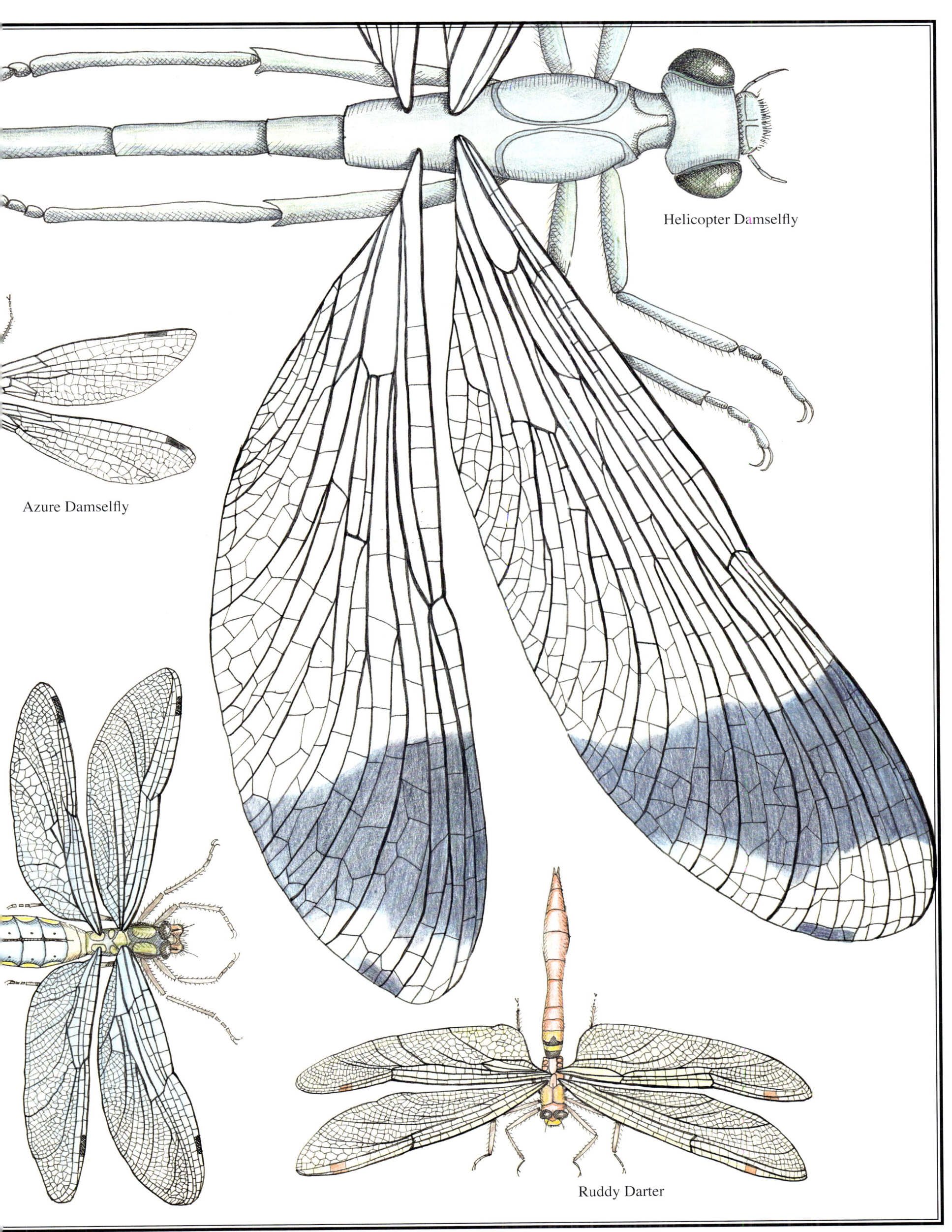

Helicopter Damselfly

Azure Damselfly

Ruddy Darter

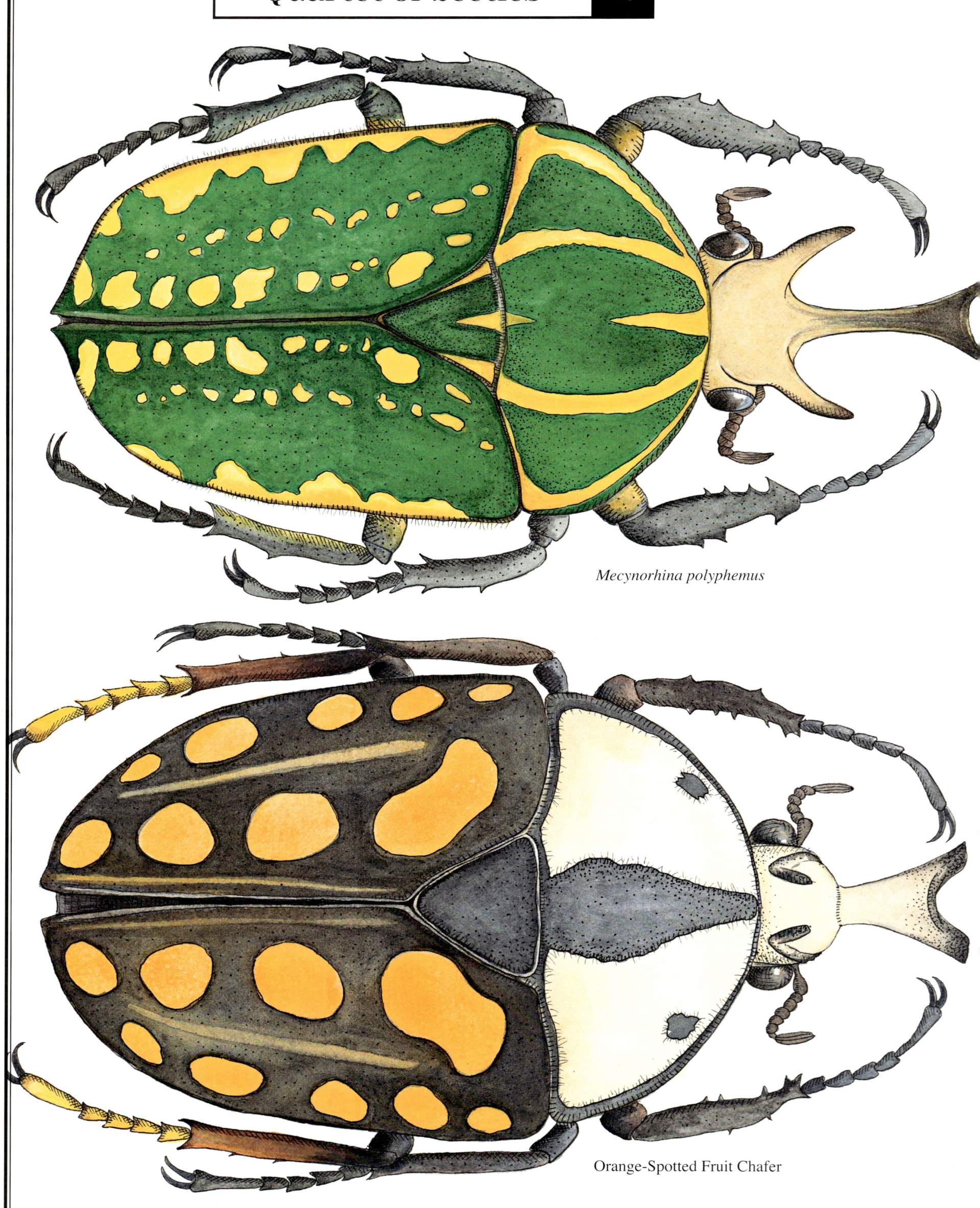

Mecynorhina polyphemus

Orange-Spotted Fruit Chafer

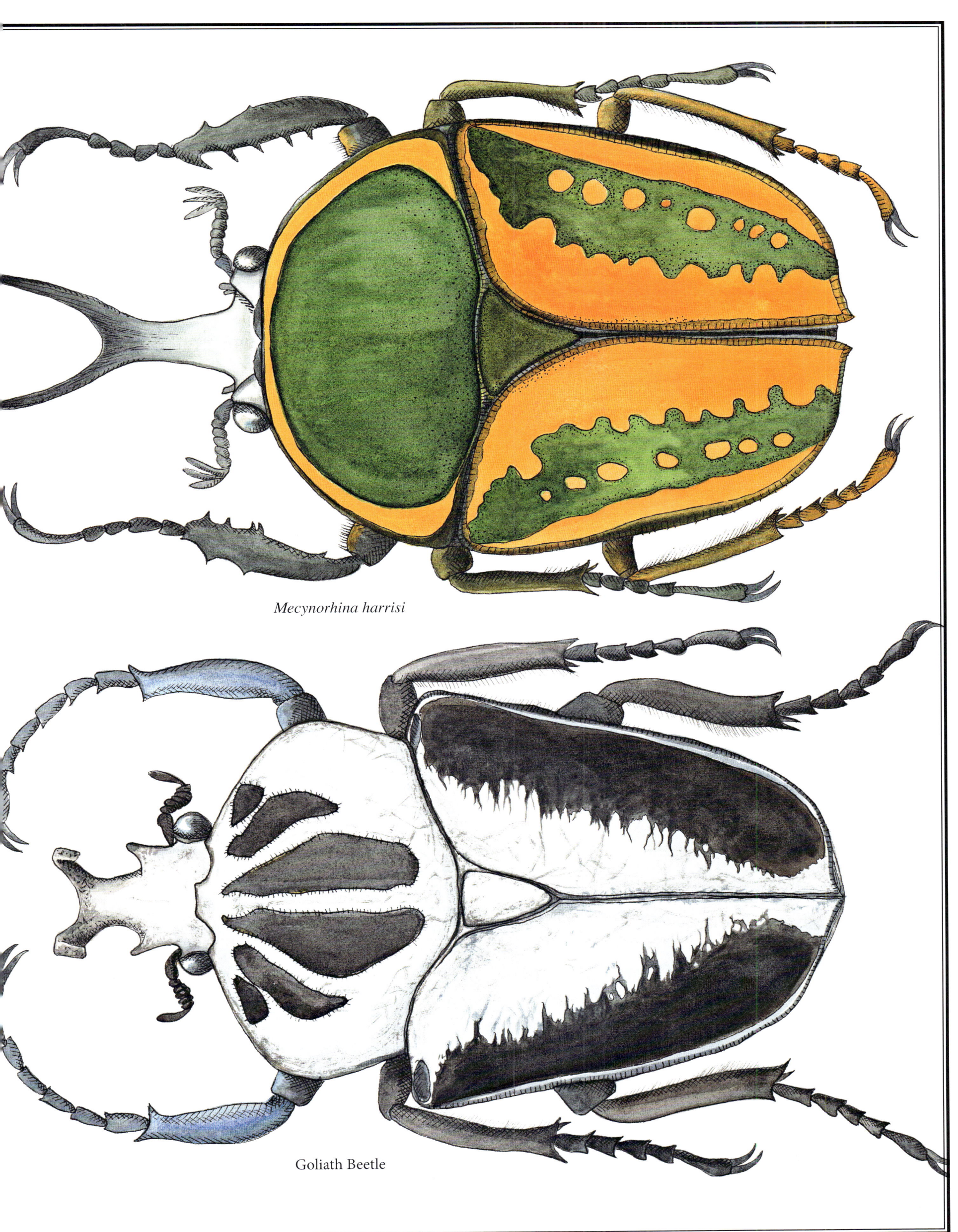

Mecynorhina harrisi

Goliath Beetle

Random Directory

Giant Leaf Insect

This species imitates leaves and, more specifically, the leaf of a guava tree. It is super-sensitive and becomes paralyzed when it senses danger, which is why it's best left undisturbed. (38)

Dead Leaf Mantis

To scare off its enemies, this mantis straightens itself into an upright position and raises its two colored legs whilst rattling its wing. It's surely an impressive sight! (39)

Amazonian Leaf Grasshopper

This is another master of camouflage. The Amazonian leaf grasshopper blends right into its environment and is amongst the least detectable creatures in the whole of nature.

Red Cabbage Shield Bug

The majority of bugs have a strong and quite unpleasant odor. It's just a defense mechanism, really, rather harmless but terribly effective. (40)

Treehopper

This creature is the perfect example of mimicry. On closer inspection, it is not a thorn, but a strange insect clung to the stem of any plant on which it feeds.

Glowworm

There's plenty of romance when this species is around, and especially at dusk, when the females transform themselves into glowing 'lanterns'. This light is produced by certain compounds in their bodies, and it will be extinguished after the males have visited. (40)

Birch Bug

This insect is just like a real-life mother hen. After laying its eggs, it settles its body on them for protection. Should predators approach, the birch bug will start to shake, flail its antennae about and even emit a smelly odor to make them leave. (40)

Tachnid Fly

Not nice at all, this little beast! The tachnid fly lays its eggs on other insects so that the larva can penetrate the skin of its host and then nibble away at it from the inside until it dies. (40)

Tiger Cactus Bug

These bugs can ravage an entire orchard of apple or pear trees, stripping the trees completely bare of leaves and fruit. (40)

Beehive Beetle

Beekeepers beware! When this fellow invades a hive, it will eat every single bee. (40)

Wireworm Harvester

This insect is a perfect acrobat. When it falls onto its back, it can actually propel itself upwards and then land back onto its feet. (41)

24-Spotted Ladybird

Gardeners love this bug! It feeds mainly on the harmful fungi that could destroy their plants. (41)

Ocellated Ladybug

Often regarded as a gardener's favorite, this large ladybug has a beast of an appetite. It can consume up to 150 aphids a day, thus eliminating insects that often destroy garden plants. (41)

Violin Beetle

To defend itself, this beetle spews out acidic and hot liquids. (41)

Southern Stalker

Dragonflies have existed for millions of years. In fact, some fossils have been found showing wingspan diameters ranging between 60 centimeters (2 feet) to 1 meter (3.3 feet).

Stone Centipede

Take good care not to touch this one! The stone centipede's bite is particularly painful. It transforms its two front legs into powerful hooks, which then eject their venom. (41)

Cockchafer Beetle

Cockroaches like this one can be eaten when they are still in larva form or when a grown insect. Native Americans roast them on open fires and eat them like popcorn. (42)

Australian Carpet Beetle

Feelers have a major role to play for all insects. They help alert insects to the presence of other insects, picking up each other's vibrations. (42/43)

Wagler's Beetle

Antennae are also used to capture smells and fragrances. They're basically the insect's nose!

Forest Giant Damselfly

The largest damselfly species, it has a wingspan of almost 20 centimeters (8 inches) and a body length of 10 centimeters (4 inches). This insect is incapable of completely folding its wings onto its back. However, it can fly at speeds of up 90 kilometers (56 miles) per hour. Not bad for such a small creature!

Azure Damselfly

This fly's eyes are huge compared to the rest of its body. One thing is for sure: the Azure has great vision. (44/45)

Emperor Dragonfly

Are you entomophagous? Put another way, would a skewer of grilled dragonflies make you begin to salivate? Well, these dragonflies are a great delicacy in Indonesia. There are, in fact, said to be between 1,700 and 2,000 species of edible insects. (44)

Guldsmed Dragonfly

This insect's huge, rotund eyes provide it with a 360 degree field of vision. (44/45)

Four-Spotted Chaser

The anterior and posterior wings of this dragonfly are unique in that they're independent of each other, enabling them to fly backwards as well as forwards. (44)

Goliath Beetle

This is one of the heaviest insects on the whole planet. Its larva alone can weigh up to 115 grams (4 ounces) and an adult insect can grow up to 10 centimeters (4 inches) in length. Goliath beetles are big favorites among insect collectors. (47)

Stick Insect

This long insect is actually used as a fishing hook in certain Asian countries and in Papua New Guinea.

Maggots

For quite a long time, these larvae were used to cure maladies. After being dropped on pus-filled wounds, maggots would eat the decomposing flesh away and simultaneously secrete chemicals that healed the wound.

Ancient Beetles

The beetle has long been associated with strength. In ancient Egypt, it symbolized the rising sun. Egyptian mummies used to be embalmed and wrapped in scarab-shaped amulets. Even today, unfortunately, they are being used as good-luck charms or jewelry.

F. Sui...

04

And now for the butterflies...

'As light as a butterfly'
Who has never heard of this expression?

Butterflies are fascinating and spectacular insects with a graceful, fleeting existence. They live everywhere except in the polar regions. The most colorful and beautiful butterflies inhabit the tropics. In temperate regions, they have come to represent spring, renewal and rebirth. Fluttering from flower to flower on a summer's day or a starry night, they invoke thoughts of freedom, carelessness and lightness. Yet, when we see a butterfly, we only witness the final stage in that insect's remarkable life. Before becoming a butterfly, the insect must undergo amazing adventures – adventures that require it to be perseverant, patient and act when the time is ripe. It all begins when a small egg is placed on a leaf. Then a tiny caterpillar comes out that will eat and eat until it has become bloated like a sponge. In fact, the caterpillar molts (or crawls out of its skin) several times as it grows and its skin becomes too tight. Next comes the making of a silk thread, with which the caterpillar rolls itself up until cocooned. Then it becomes a chrysalis, which will finally lead to that much anticipated moment everyone is eager to see: the entrance, or, should we say, departure of the butterfly! Yet, is the fate of the butterfly more enviable that that of the caterpillar? It flies and swirls, its shimmering colors attract everyone's attention, seducing them with their incredible patterns. Indeed, certain butterfly collectors admire them so much that they don't hesitate to apply their specimens with chloroform (a chemical that prevents the wings from molding) and then frame them on their living room walls. Sadly, it seems that butterflies are becoming more scarce the world over. Nature exists without humans, yet it would seem that the reverse is rather difficult. To prevent these beautiful insects from becoming extinct, let's forget the 'butterfly chase' and just be happy to observe them. Let's capture them through our binoculars or with our cameras. Let it not be forgotten that butterflies add value to our ecosystem and are a true, quality 'brand' of our natural environment.

Madagascan Sunset Moth

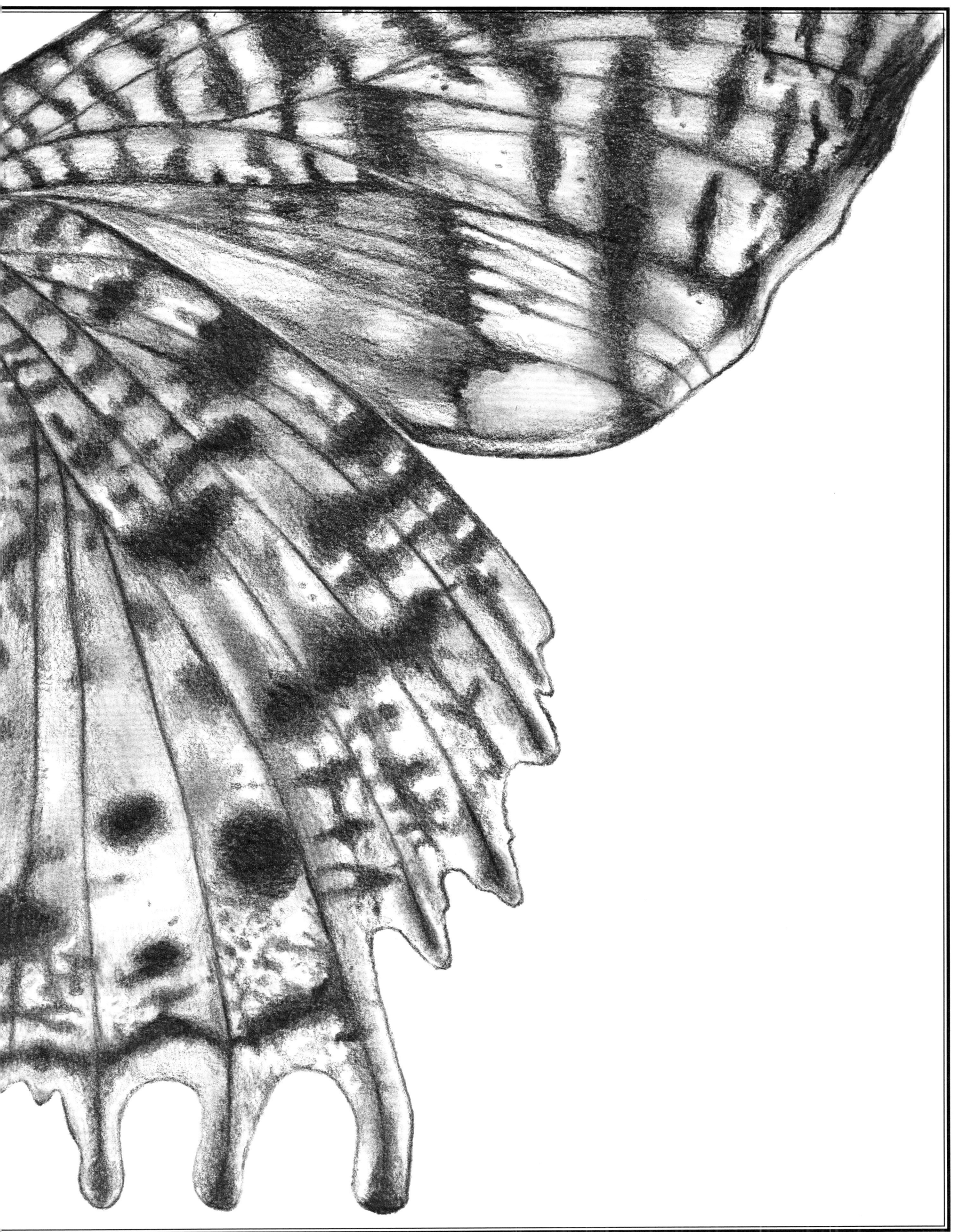

Owl Butterfly

Comet Moth

Hieroglyph Moth

Dalman Tiger

Atlas Moth

Shepherd's Footman

Cinnabar Moth

Death's-Head Hawkmoth

Isabella

Leopard Moth

Miller

Red Underwing

Garden Tiger Moth

Leprieur's Glory

Large Green-Banded Blue

Ornithopter Moth

Blue Cracker

Hewitson Hairstreak

Tanzanian Tiara

Memphis moruus

Common Blue

Apollo Metalmark

Giant Blue Swallowtail

Blue Pansy

Blue Wave Tropical

Helena Morpho

Brilliant Blue

Random Directory

Ceylan
Take a closer look! The wings of this butterfly resemble an impressionist painting. The color strokes are like tiny fish scales or roof tiles, which when put together form magnificent geometric designs.

Leopard Moth
Moths fly in accordance with the moon's movements. Not all of them fly at the same time, and some prefer either twilight or the very darkest night. Others even wait until dawn to move. (55)

Owl Butterfly
When its wings are outspread, this insect can look quite scary. It seems as if an owl or other night bird is looking at you. As a master of camouflage with its false owl eyes, it can fly away and escape from enemies instead of becoming their little snack. (54)

Dalman Tiger
Butterflies have a thin trunk for a mouth. They use it like a straw, sucking nectar from flowers or sap from trees. The Dalman tiger likes crushed apple juice. Some moths even feed on the blood of injured animals. (54)

Atlas Moth
This beauty's wingspan is about 30 centimeters (1 foot) long, making it one of the biggest butterflies in the world. There is a design at the tip of its wings that looks like a snake's head, which is why the Atlas is also known as the Cobra butterfly. (54)

Garden Tiger Moth
Resting and with wings closed, this insect hides the striking red color of its hind wings. But the moment it is attacked, it opens them wide and the surprised aggressor gets scared and flees. (55)

Cinnabar Moth
All owls beware and take off! This moth tastes awful. It's actually poisonous, and its toxicity is a result of the leaves it ate as a caterpillar. (55)

Death's-Head Hawkmoth
This species originates from Africa and is a great traveler. It's capable of flying more than 3,000 kilometers (1,860 miles), as far as Iceland or even Russia. (55)

Isabella
When Lady Isabella releases chemicals called pheromones in the early morning, males from far and wide are attracted to arrive and mate. And that gathering may last for several hours. (55)

Forest Giant Owl
This species is one of the largest and most spectacular owl butterflies!

Miller
Together with the Atlas butterfly, the Miller's 30 centimeter (1 foot) wingspan makes it one of the biggest in the world. It is also called the 'White Witch' and sometimes gets mistaken for a bat. (55)

Red Underwing
Undercover operation! The big red wings of this butterfly are hidden by the hind legs when it is resting. (54/55)

Hieroglyph Moth
Moths have tympanal organs that can detect sound waves called ultrasound, which are too high in pitch for people to hear. These insects use their special hearing to detect and escape from enemies, just as bats do. (54)

Blue Morpho
Colored a metallic, fluorescent, reflective blue, this beautiful insect is the delight of all butterfly collectors, or lepidopterists as they prefer to be known.

Blue Night Moth

Butterfly and moth wings consist of numerous tiny scales. The insects can use their wings to secrete odors that attract mates.

Ornithopter Moth

'Ornithopter' is the name for both a large butterfly and a flying machine inspired by the flapping of huge wings. Whilst Leonardo da Vinci was the first to imagine this machine more than 500 years ago, it has yet to be built. But it is still a dream for many lovers of flight! (56)

Blue Cracker

The color of butterflies is often determined by what the caterpillar ate prior to metamorphosis. Our eyes can see the butterfly's colors when sunlight is reflected off the surface of the animal's scales. For species with iridescent coloring, the hues we see will change depending on the angle from which we look at the insect. British researchers actually managed to recreate the complex structure of the wing of a butterfly, using scales piled up like tiles on a roof. There may be a use for this structure in banknote production. It could make it harder to produce counterfeit money and prevent fraud. (56)

Memphis moruus

Butterflies are able to recognize one another thanks to the patterning and colors of their wings. They can detect colors humans can see, as well as those that are only visible in ultraviolet light. (56)

Tanzanian Tiara

Make sure not to touch a butterfly's wings. If you do, you'll find a fine powder in your fingers. This represents some of the animal's scales you've just removed, which means you've also removed some of the color, too. (56)

Common Blue

Butterflies symbolize rebirth in some ancient texts. And in some legends, the soul of the deceased is reincarnated into the butterfly. (57)

Apollo Metalmark

The flight of butterflies can be either slow or very fast. Researchers study the details of how they move, in order to come up with new ideas for improved flying machines. (57)

Southern Swallowtail

Flight will always depend on the type of wings in question. Those butterflies with a large wing surface area are able to travel further, just like a glider, and without the need to flap too frequently.

Hewitson Hairstreak

The number of butterfly and moth species at night far exceeds those during the day. There are 140,000 night flyers for every 20,000 day trippers! (56/57)

Common Morpho

This pretty butterfly is fairly unpopular in the Amazon regions of Peru. Natives there believe it embodies evil spirits because its bright, iridescent wings disorientate travelers that venture into the jungle.

Blue Wave Tropical

When a butterfly is attracted by the fragrance of a flower, it first tastes the bloom using the hair covering its legs. Then, it unrolls the trunk wrapped around its head and samples the nectar. Trunk lengths vary from a few centimeters to over 30 centimeters (1 foot). One of the largest trunks belongs to the Morgan's Sphinx moth of Madagascar, which uses it to pollinate very deeply into certain orchid flowers. (56/57)

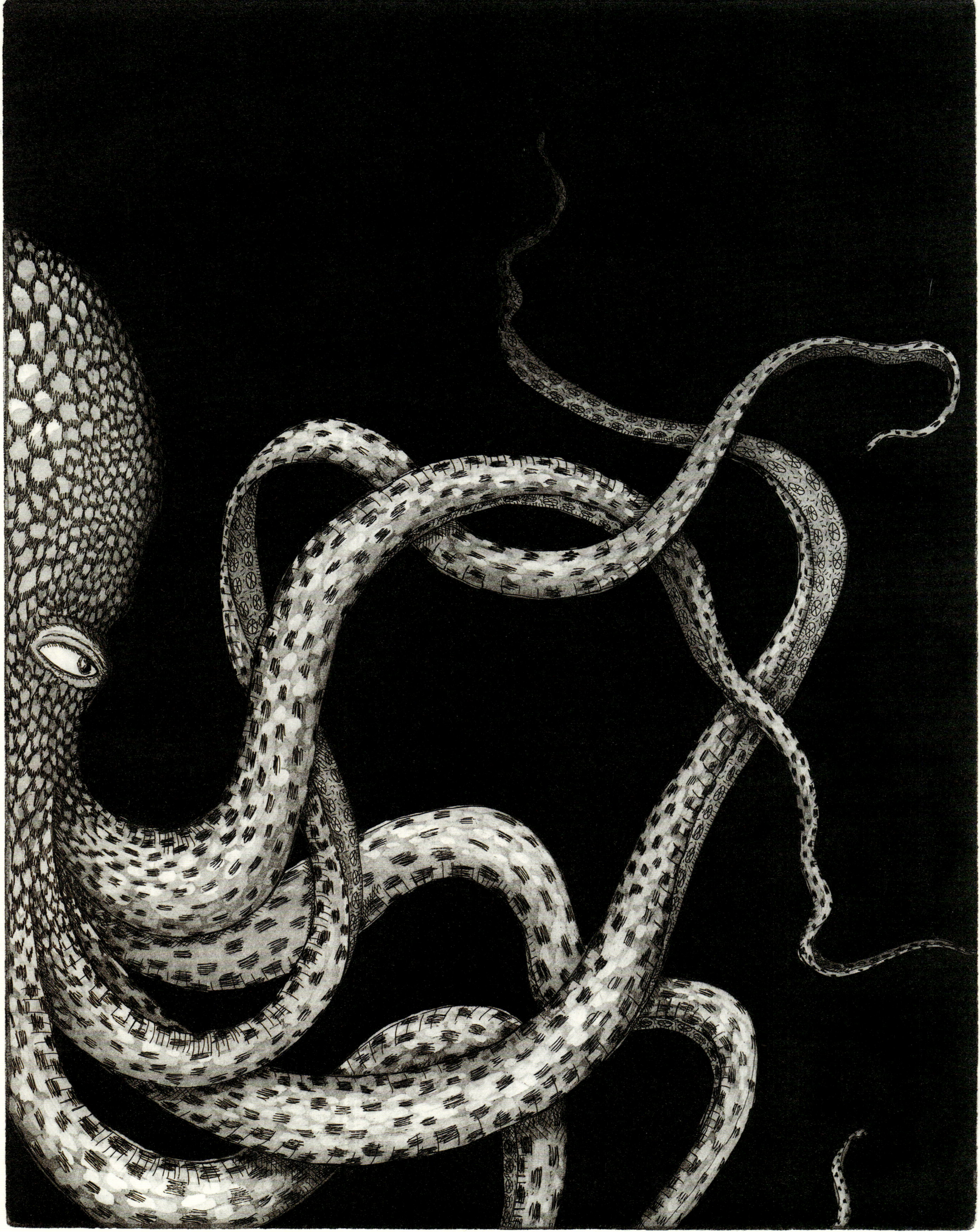

7/15   F. Guiz...

05

Natural sailors

No limits, no boundaries.

This fauna, evolved in water, stuns all onlookers and gives the impression that it's without limit or boundary. Everything in the underwater world seems to slide along: the octopuses and their monstrous tentacles, the brittle stars with their gracious ballet dance routines or the light shuffle of sea urchins. It's not necessary to be a professional diver to understand the sense of intoxication even seasoned divers talk about when they have gone 20 meters (65 feet) into the deep. What caught my surprise was the diversity of these marine environments, whose species are more incredible than those found in other places. Oceans account for about 70% of the Earth's surface area. As far as we now know, the deepest underwater point lies 11,034 meters (36,200 feet) below the ocean surface. This place is in the northern Pacific, just off the Marianas archipelago. It took over 2 and a half hours to descend to that point using the best diving equipment. Did you know, however, that these vast depths represent 90% of the ocean and only 1% of it has been researched to date? The immensity of these unknown, undiscovered 'countries' is hard to imagine. In the marine environment, everything is about interaction. Grave consequences occur when the environment is disturbed for whatever reason – and that disturbance is usually caused by humans. After being introduced by people, giant crabs have invaded the Norwegian coastline and are threatening native sea life. Other human-related activities, such as global warming and overfishing, have helped cause jellyfish populations to swell and damage marine environments around the world. Nonetheless, there is room for optimism because nature has powerful defense mechanisms. But enough about ecological problems – let us wonder at these curious living beauties of the sea.

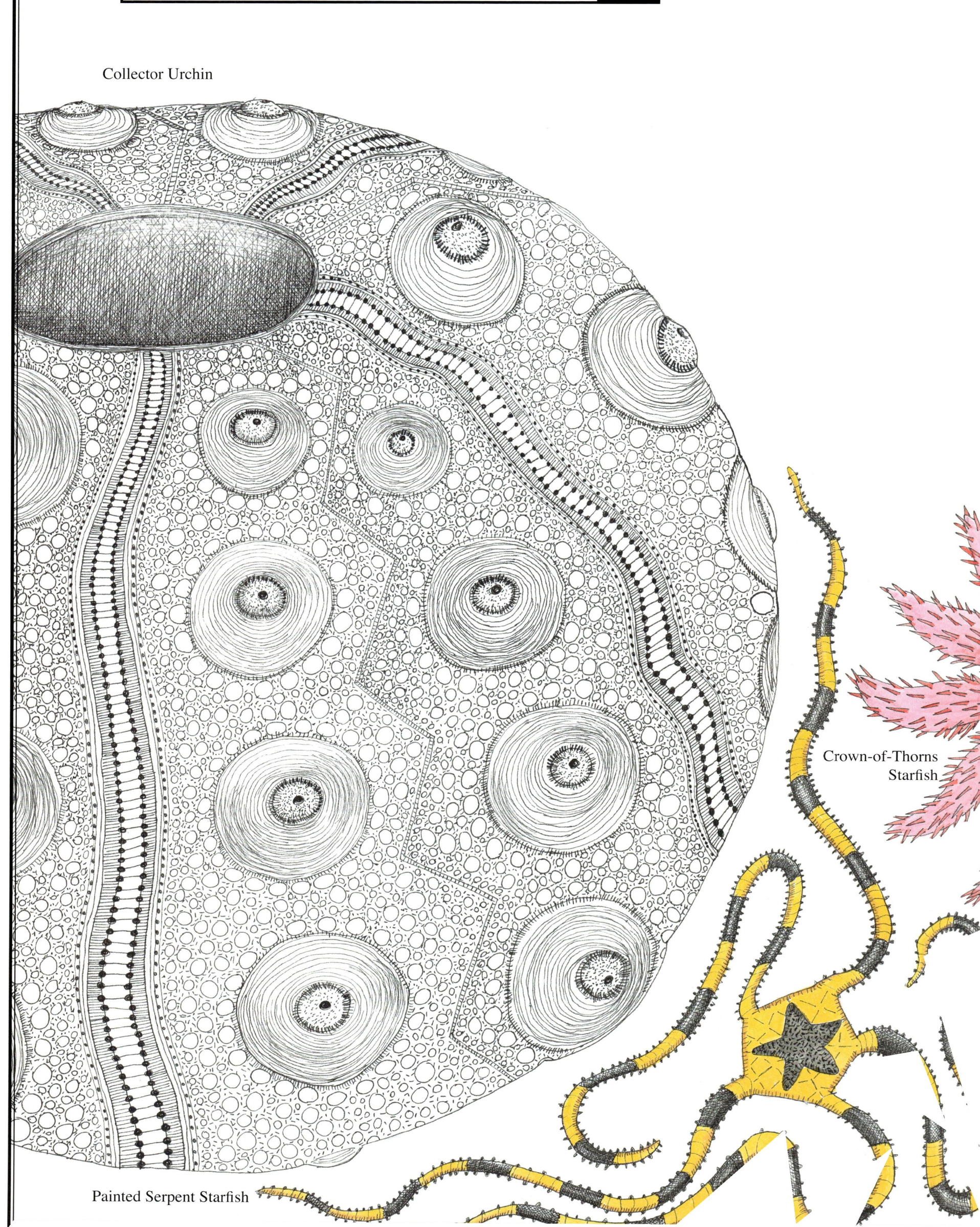

Collector Urchin

Crown-of-Thorns
Starfish

Painted Serpent Starfish

Sunflower Sea Star

Peltaster placenta

Blue Linckia Starfish

Tan Starfish

Hurghada Star

Common Brittle Star

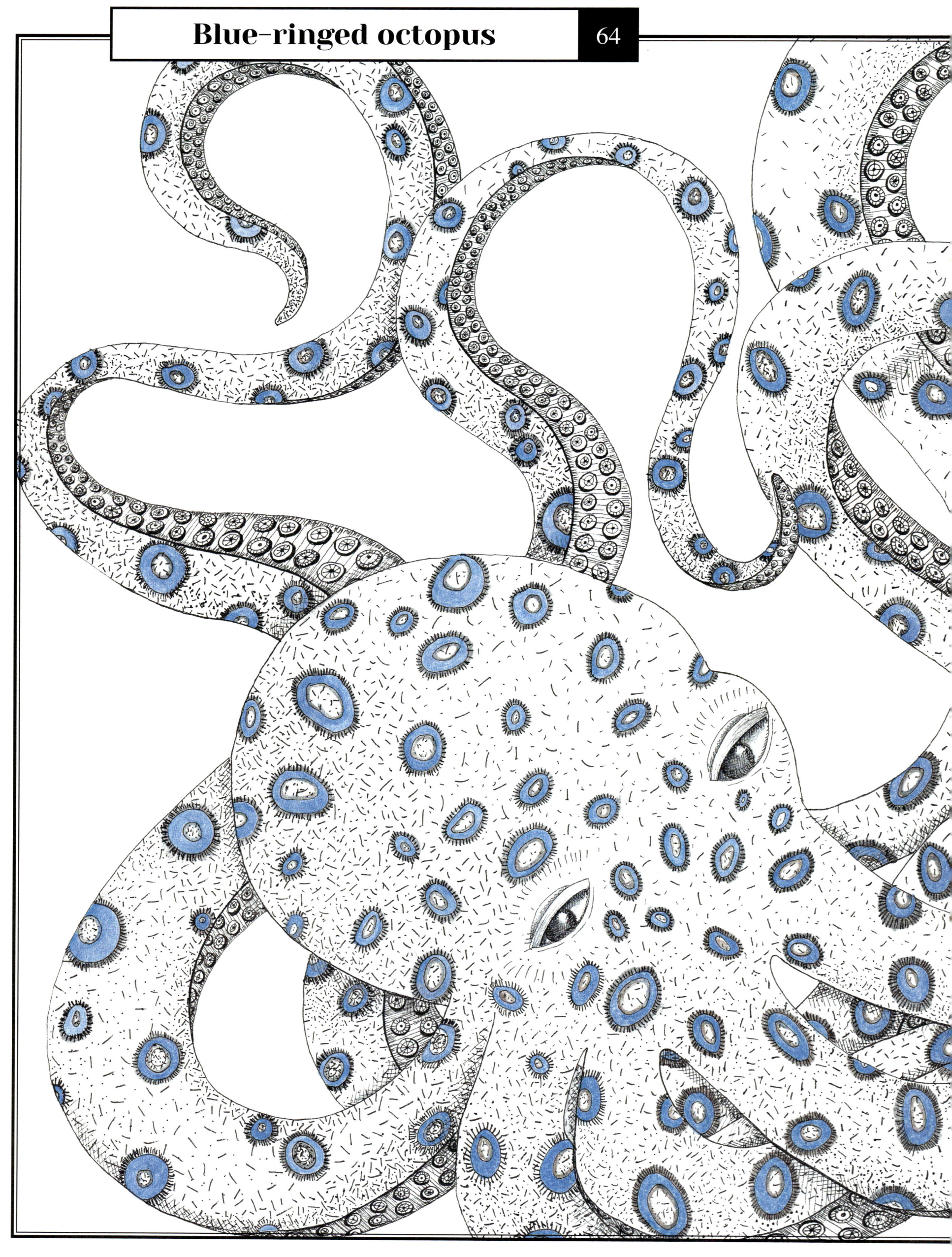

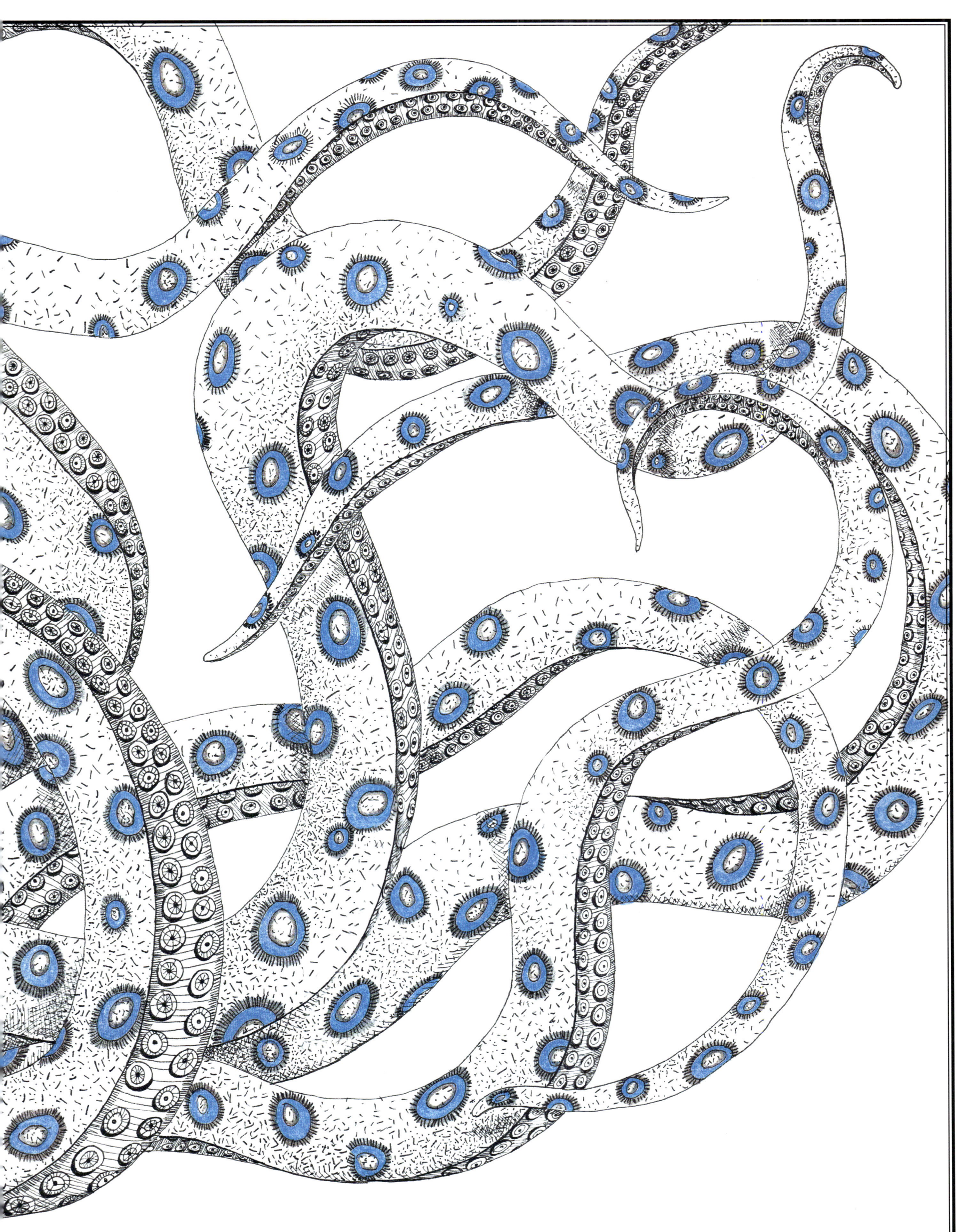

Spider Crab

Spiny Lobster

Spotted Reef Crab

Spotted Coral Crab

Lobster

Random Directory

Collector Urchin

This spiny urchin has a hard, rock-like shell for protection. It's also the creature we pick up stranded on the beach, dead and having lost its spines. (62)

Common Sea Urchin

It's the hedgehog of the seas! Contrary to common belief, this urchin does not move with its spines alone, but also with many, many little suction pads on its arms. It's a herbivore and grazes on algae. One of its biggest enemies is the starfish, which enjoys its flesh.

Sand Dollar

This is a flat type of sea urchin buried under the sand. Its spines are very short and almost fur-like. When it dies, all that remains is its shell. The five-pointed star on its round, flat body is absolutely perfect, a marvel of structure and design. Some people think the animal looks like an old dollar coin, which is why it's called the sand dollar.

Sunflower Sea Star

What a strange creature! It is born with five branches, but the number goes on to become twenty-four, each one identical as the animal grows and grows. In addition, it's the fastest of all the starfish, able to move at about 3.6 kilometers (2.2 miles) per hour, which is the same speed as a human child. (63)

Blue Linckia Starfish

This starfish is so beautiful that nobody will leave it alone. It's as prized by 'ecotourists', who search it out while scuba diving, as it is by the tourists who buy it stuffed as a souvenir at the seaside shops. (63)

Spiny Cushion Star

When young, this species is flat and pentagon shaped, but during growth it plumps up and adopts the circular shape of a cushion.

Tan Starfish

Like all marine stars, this one is a night owl, moving about at nighttime in search of food. (63)

Hurghada Star

This is a mini star, no bigger than 8 centimeters (3.1 inches). It is a 'protandrous hermaphrodite', starting life as a male and changing to a female. (63)

Crown-of-Thorns Starfish

This is the only starfish that's toxic. It's also a terrible enemy to coral reef environments. In 2009, in the area around the Moorea Island in French Polynesia, the Corwn-of-Thorns managed to eat away at 98% of the coral. With a diameter length of up to 60 centimeters (24 inches), this attractive but dangerous animal becomes enormous and its spines poisonous to humans. (62/63)

New Zealand Cushion Star

This flat, five-sided starfish has a clever way of hunting. It arches upwards on the tip of its arms to form an alcove to attract its prey. Once inside, its lunch is captured by simply closing its arms again.

Purple Serpent Star

With a forest of extremely sharp, 12 centimeter (5 inch) long spines covering its five arms, this creature is truly impressive. Fortunately, it is not venomous.

Common Brittle Star

A cousin of the starfish, this creature can live in the lowest depths of the ocean – up to 4,000 meters (13,000 feet) deep, in fact. With its long arms, its only way to move about is by shuffling itself along. (63)

Blue-Ringed Octopus

Such a beauty, and dangerous to boot! Make sure not to annoy this deadly creature. Despite its small size, the blue-ringed octopus possesses an absolutely lethal venom, capable of killing humans. Normally, it's colored beige; but as soon as is senses danger, blue rings appear on its body to show predators how dangerous it can be. (64/65)

Lobster

Up to the nineteenth century, insects and crustaceans were actually thought to be closely related because they both had antennae. The lobster's antennae help it move about. When alerting its companions of imminent danger, it uses the antennae to produce a sound as if a bow were striking violin strings. (67)

Spider Crab

When they migrate, spider crabs move in their hundreds, like an army of foot soldiers. These huge crab swarms often create an impressive pyramid shape. Gifted with great talents in the art of disguise, spider crabs use seaweed, sponge and other algae to hide themselves. This trait is perfect for camouflage. After cutting up these materials, the crab impregnates them with an adhesive saliva and then sticks it on its shell. (66/67)

Spotted Reef Crab

What a pretty crab this one is, with its red spots! Philatelists (or stamp collectors) love it, too. Spotted reef crabs have been featured on at least a dozen postage stamps from countries in the Pacific region. (66)

Spotted Coral Crab

Do you know the Japanese contemporary artist Yayoi Kusama? All his paintings, sculptures and installations are made out of peas – they are his trademark. This little crab, with its pea-like markings, could be one of Kusama's artworks! (67)

Burrowing Urchin

In order to conceal themselves, burrowing urchins can dig holes into very hard rocks. Urchin-made cavities have even been discovered in the stonework of pillars.

Mimic Octopus

This octopus has an extraordinary ability to transform itself into many things. To help avoid its predators, it can take on the form of a dozen different species, including anemones, snakes, jellyfish and moray eels. It's an underwater chameleon!

E.A

06

More underwater beauties

A family that was hard to classify

For centuries, people did not understand exactly what coral was. Some thought it was a mineral, while others classified it as a plant. It wasn't until a British scientist named William Herschel (1738–1822) studied coral samples under a microscope – and he determined once and for all that it was actually a marine animal. What previously had been deemed to be the cup of a flower was now seen to be an animal's body. This discovery left many scientists of the time bewildered, and it took quite a long time to be fully validated and accepted. So it's no wonder that even in modern times, coral is thought of as plant life forming the 'garden' of the ocean, sumptuously decorated with its multicolored 'flower beds'. When we dive down into these lavish, harmonious coral environments, our vision is not able to decipher what it sees as it could on land. Range is altered and our perception underwater is different. There is an explosion of colors and shapes, not to mention occurrences. Who would not be amazed by the ballet of a crystal jellyfish? Fauna, flora and other surprises are everywhere. The spectacle of the most prominent reef on Earth, the Great Barrier Reef, is of exceptional beauty – both from above and below. Together with our rain forests, this coral reef system is one of the richest natural areas on the planet, a true ecosystem and the result of hundreds of millions of years of evolution. It's home to a diversity of species that have mutually established a very sophisticated and intimate alliance. Today, however, these magical places are threatened by climate change and human activity – threats that could lead to their complete disappearance.

Button Coral

Flower Pot Coral

Sun Coral

Mushroom Coral

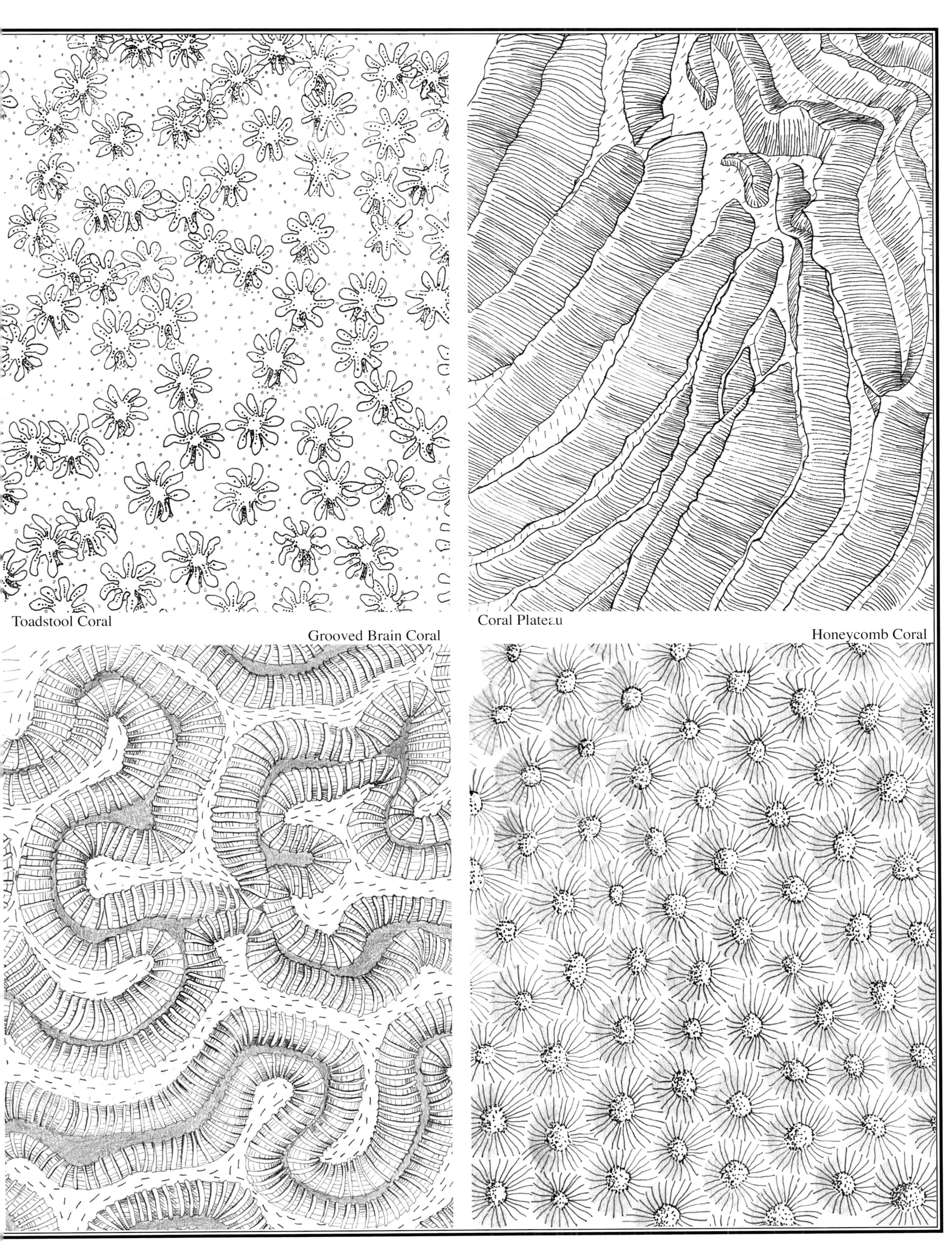

Toadstool Coral

Coral Plateau

Grooved Brain Coral

Honeycomb Coral

Portuguese Man 'o War

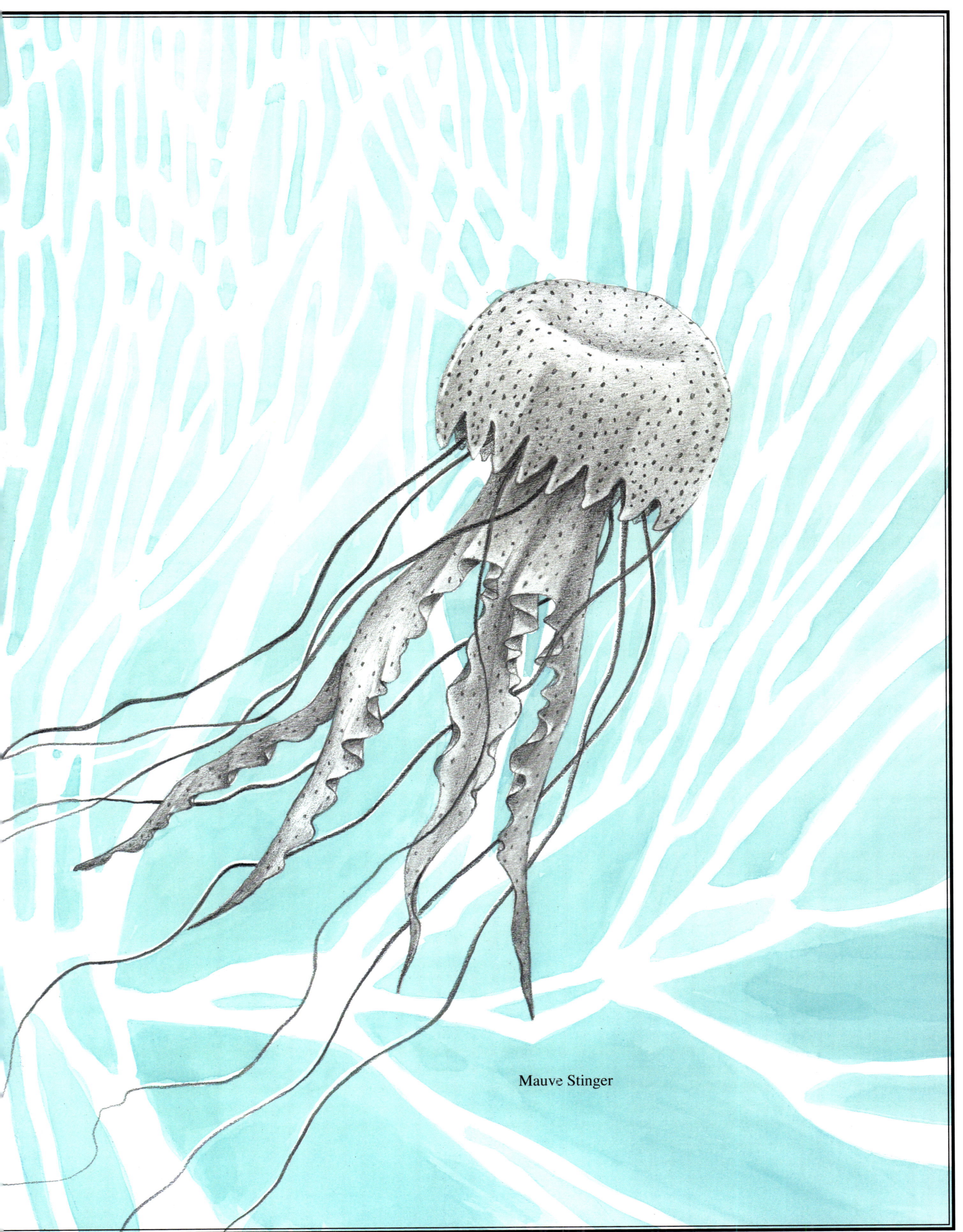

Mauve Stinger

Giant Sea Fan

Lyre Coral

Pink Noded Horny Coral

Orange Sea Lily

Delicate Sea Whip

Comatulids

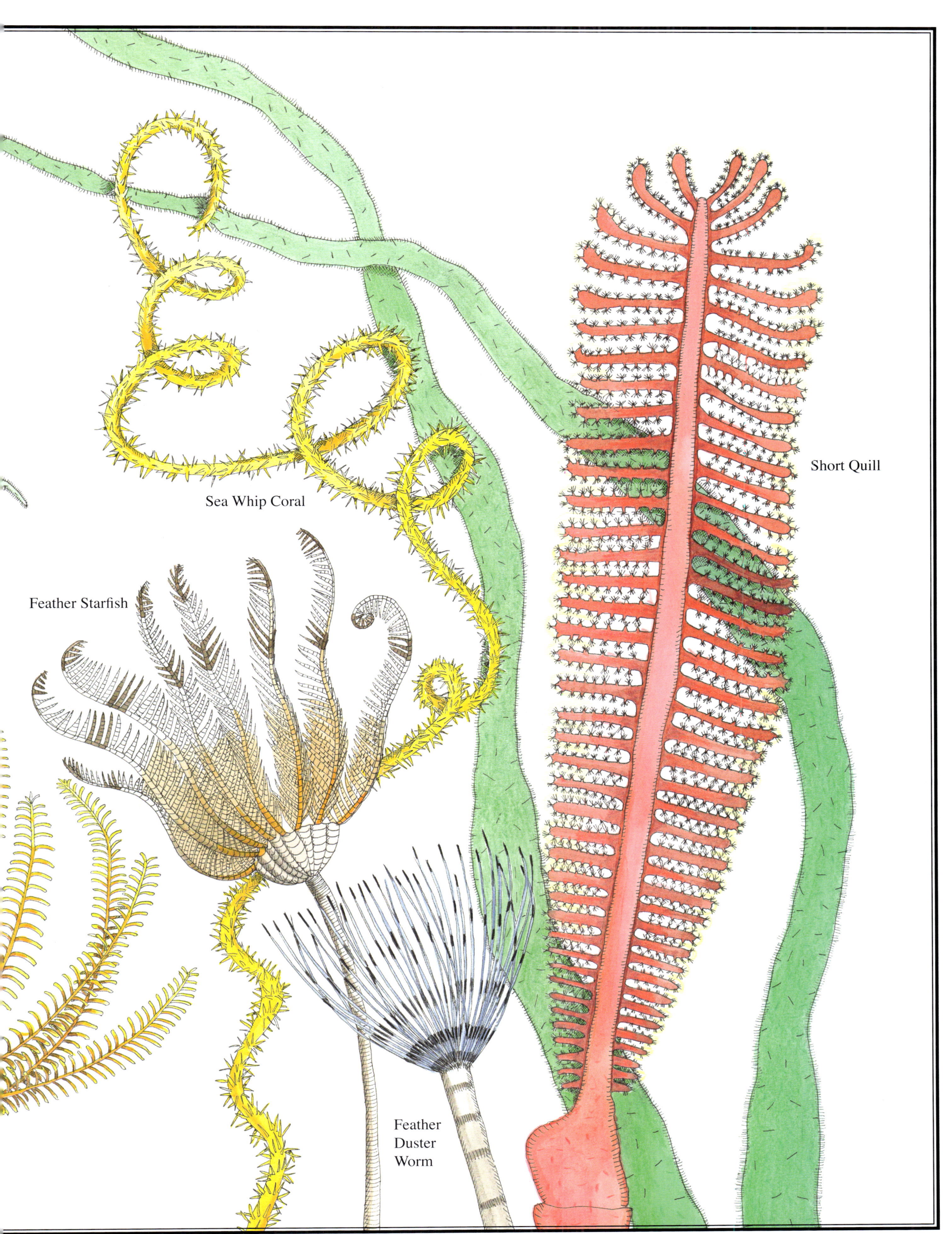

Sea Whip Coral

Short Quill

Feather Starfish

Feather
Duster
Worm

Random Directory

Coral Builder

This is a strange creature: an animal called a polyp. It's tubed-shaped, stands on a base and has arms and branches reaching to the other end. It lives in a limestone skeleton, just like a snail lives in its shell. You might also call this creature the coral builder. When it dies, its outer skeleton remains and other generations of coral are able to develop it further. It is the continuous accumulation of these limestone exoskeletons, together with seaweed and bits of shell, that forms the coral reef.

Coral Reef

Corals are the basic elements of all reefs: they provide shelter to a vast number of species. They are a true asylum for crustaceans, fish and sponges of all types – a world of total 'symbiosis', where all skills are shared.

The Great Barrier Reef of Australia

This is the largest barrier reef in the world, more than 2,000 kilometers (1,240 miles) long. The Great Barrier Reef ecosystem has existed for thousands of years.

Great Threats

Pacific corals are under great threat. They have fallen victim to a formidable thorny sea star that's already destroyed great numbers of coral reefs.

Bleaching

All corals around the world are affected by this threat. Due to water temperatures rising, tiny algae – those providing color – are losing their nutrients. The result is widespread bleaching.

Cyclones

By pure force of its waves, a cyclone can destroy everything in its path, and that includes anything 30 meters (100 feet) deep! Even though nature has a remarkable ability to regenerate itself, several years are required to rebuild these maritime environments.

Button Coral

The button coral's maze-like surface resembles a brain, but it's wise not to touch this large creature because it stings. (72)

Portuguese Man 'o War

This creature is puffed up with gas and looks just like a miniature sailboat. If ever an enemy were to show up, it simply deflates itself and then stings from below the surface. Unbelievable! (74)

Mauve Stinger

This pretty jellyfish is phosphorescent. It's beautiful to see when you're scuba diving at night, but take care when getting close up. Its tentacles can cause extremely serious burns. (75)

Medusa or Common Jellyfish

The name Medusa was given to this creature because of its tentacles, which closely resemble the hair of the ancient gorgon (or sea monster) named Medusa – one of three such gorgons in ancient Greek mythology.

Lion's Mane Jellyfish

This is the biggest jellyfish of all. It has a canopy of two and half meters (8.2 feet), which at full stretch looks like a fully opened umbrella…

An Easy Meal

Some jellyfish swim backwards, looking like a salad bowl. Plankton, the animals' main food, simply drops down right into their empty mouths!

On the Menu...

So who eats jellyfish, anyway? Some fish do, as well as some birds, but it's the turtle who especially likes jellyfish. The leatherback sea turtle has a fondness for the squishy creature. And, of course, so do humans: in Asia, jellyfish are sliced and eaten in salads, as well as dried or even grilled in skewers.

The Fountain of Youth

The gelatinous body of jellyfish actually contains a substance called collagen. Cosmetics labs have long exploited jellyfish collagen to manufacture their anti-wrinkle creams

The Sea Wasp

This is the most poisonous jellyfish on record, often killing its prey over a period of hours. It has sixty tentacles, each laden with venom and capable of being extended up to 4 meters (13 feet)!

Short Quill

It's hard to believe, but this 'feather' is actually a living creature, able to eat, reproduce and move about. (79)

Feather Duster Worm

Actually, this is not a feather duster, but a worm that inhabits a cylindrical tube embedded in the sand. On being approached, it simply retracts into its shell. (79)

Feather Starfish

This animal, a type of crinoid, feeds itself using its articulated arms. Many crinoids are contained in fossils, meaning they existed in prehistoric times. (79)

Sea Whip Coral

This one often looks like a long, spiraling piece of iron. It's covered by thorns and just floats with the surf. (79)

Sea Fern

To feed itself, this fern spreads its arms out like a fan, captures its prey, and then channels it through its long feathers toward its awaiting mouth. When it's had enough to eat, it simply folds its arms back around itself.

Comatulids

This plant-like creature has articulated fingers shaped in a bunch, which enable it to traipse along. It moves very slowly, and it grips onto anything it can use as a support. (78)

Delicate Sea Whip

Who would think that this mass of big stems is actually a type of coral? Known as soft coral, it is very supple and tilts as though its head were leaning. This coral sways a lot, and its tiny little polyps make it look as if it's a flowering garden. (78)

Alcyonacea

This coral type comes alive at night, when it can be seen spreading and swinging its long stems lustfully as the current flows. It looks similar to a large tree swaying in the wind.

Lyre Coral

With its long, parallel branches, this coral resembles a lyre or a comb. It could even be the comb of a sea siren... (76/77)

Giant Sea Fan

This one really is a giant. Its outstretched tails can reach 3 meters (9.8 feet). (76)

Pink Noded Horny Coral

This pretty coral has white, flower-shaped polyps that are in sharp contrast to the red of its branches. Whenever there is a sign of danger, the whole coral gets the message and the polyps on the branch retract. (77)

07

A festival of fish

Are fish communities all that different from humans ones?

Why are fish less loved by us than mammals? Well, they live in water, are cold to the touch, breathe completely differently from humans and, above all, do not show their emotions. Moreover, their world is not particularly accessible to us. Going out to discover ocean creatures requires real drive – boats need to be hired and special diving equipment needs to be prepared and used. In some parts of the sea, especially the ocean floor, human exploration is almost impossible. Maybe these are some of the reasons why we don't have the same attachment to fish that we do to warm blooded animals. Maybe we would like to communicate with them? But who has ever heard or tried to understand the voice of a fish?

Nonetheless, fish are extraordinary creatures to study. There are more than 30,000 species living in the seas and oceans, and new ones are still being discovered. The biggest is the whale shark, which can measure up to 15 meters (50 feet); while the smallest, the dwarf goby, is barely 8 millimeters (0.3 inch) long. Some fish, including the barracuda, can zoom about like torpedoes. Others can only traipse awkwardly across the earth, like the little mudspringer. One species hid itself so well in the sea that people thought it was extinct. For centuries, paleontologists only knew about the giant coelacanth fish from ancient fossils. Then in 1938, a living specimen was discovered off the coast of South Africa. A 'dead' species had come to life! Such discoveries inspire curiosity and amazement, even though we may not feel as close to fish as we do to dogs and cats. As Madame de Staël stated in the 18th century, 'The spectacle of the sea always makes a deep impression. It is vast, it is the image of the infinite, which is a permanent cause for contemplation and in which it could be lost forever'.

Hawkfish

White-Spotted Boxfish

Blue-Ringed Angelfish

Sixbar Wrasse

Emperor Angelfish

Six-Line Wrasse

Opah

Coral Hind

Blacksaddled
Coral Grouper

Mandarinfish

Clown Triggerfish

Heniochus

Pajama Cardinalfish

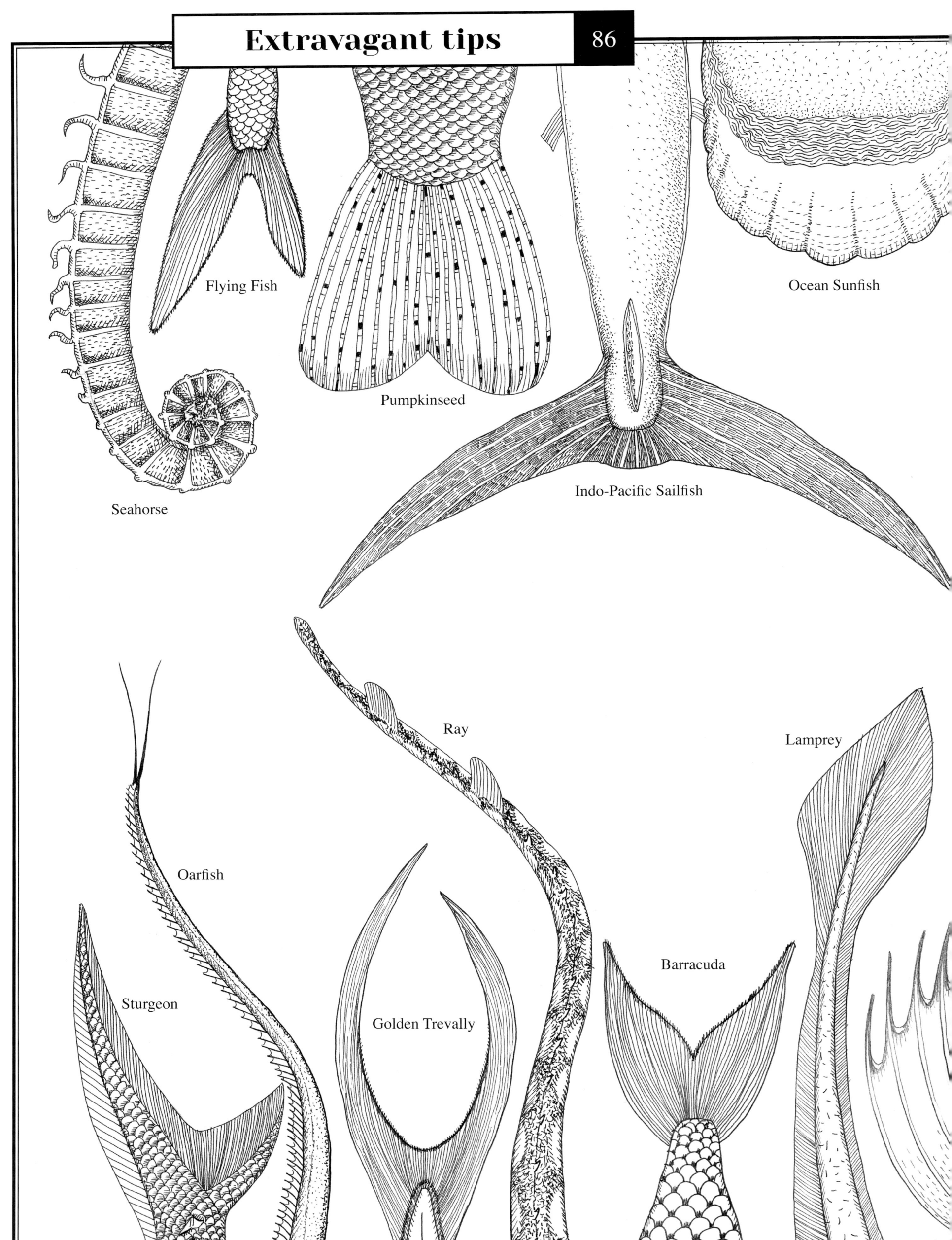

Seahorse

Flying Fish

Pumpkinseed

Indo-Pacific Sailfish

Ocean Sunfish

Ray

Lamprey

Oarfish

Sturgeon

Golden Trevally

Barracuda

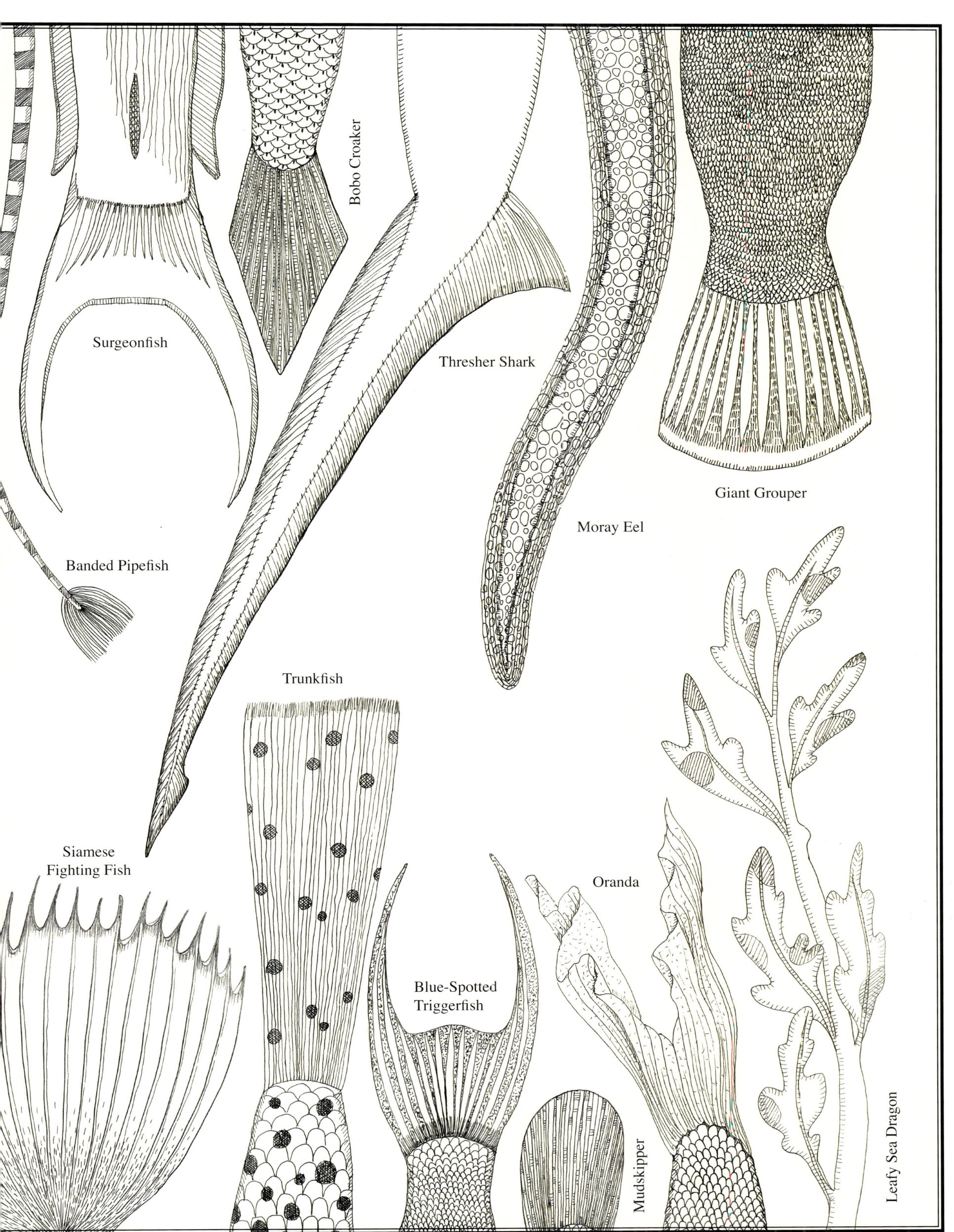

Surgeonfish

Bobo Croaker

Thresher Shark

Moray Eel

Giant Grouper

Banded Pipefish

Trunkfish

Siamese
Fighting Fish

Blue-Spotted
Triggerfish

Oranda

Mudskipper

Leafy Sea Dragon

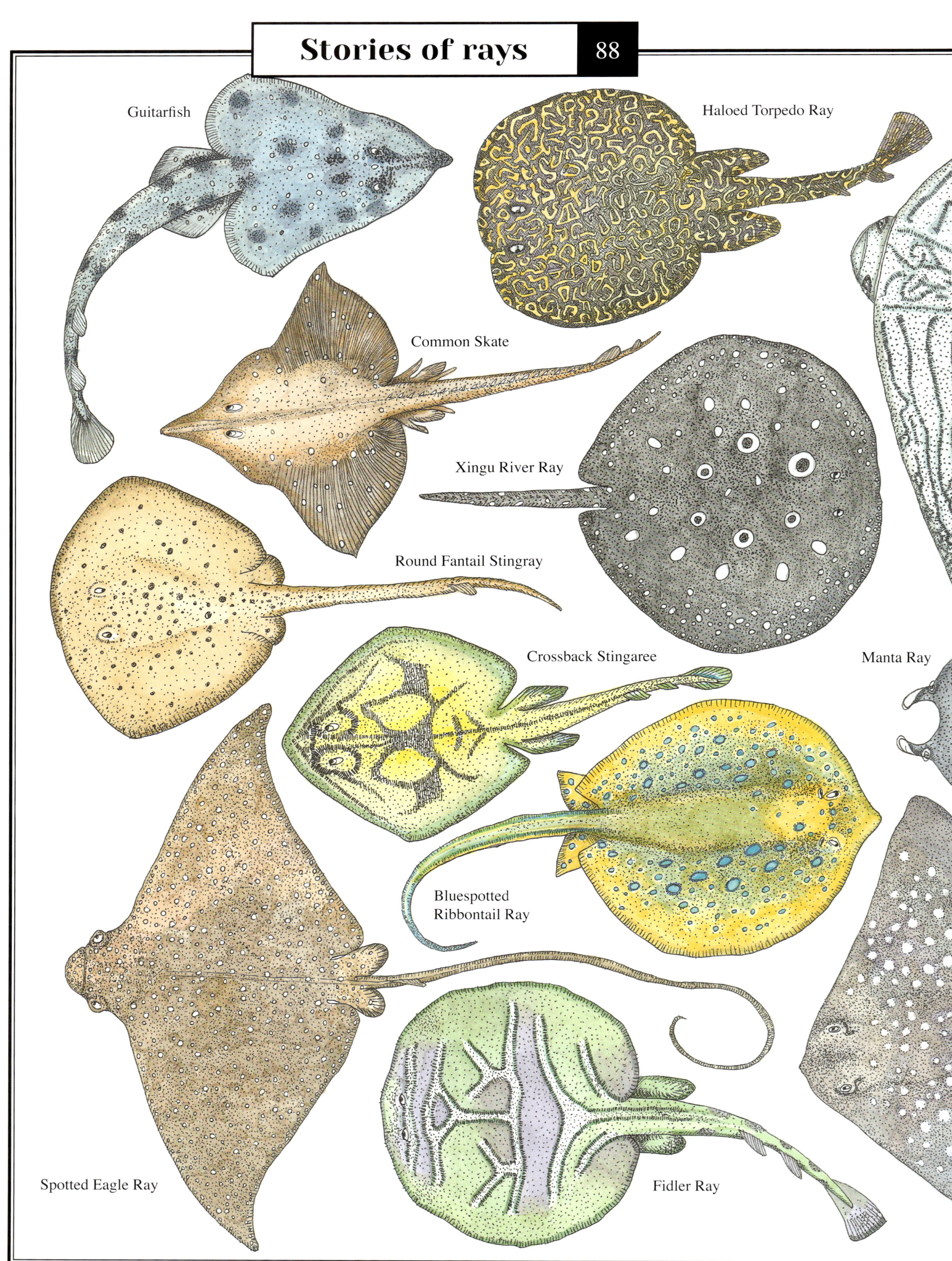

Guitarfish

Haloed Torpedo Ray

Common Skate

Xingu River Ray

Round Fantail Stingray

Crossback Stingaree

Manta Ray

Bluespotted
Ribbontail Ray

Spotted Eagle Ray

Fidler Ray

Ornate Eagle Ray

Blue Skate

Thorny Skate

Bullseye Round Stingray

Circular Stingaree

Undulate Ray

Butterfly Ray

Brazilian Electric Ray

Reticulate Whipray

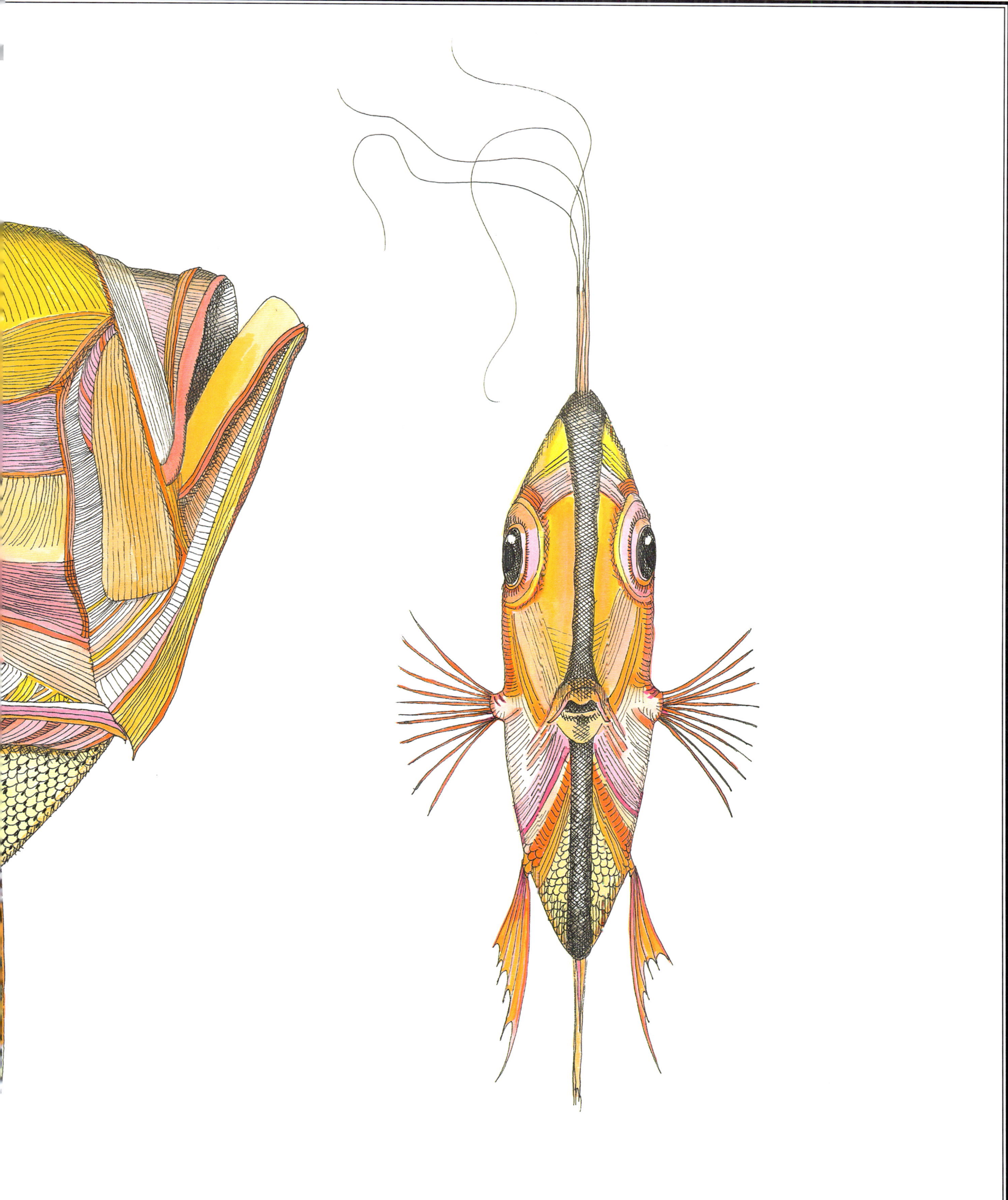

Random Directory

Hawkfish
This fish oozes elegance whilst swimming through the coral and algae, a colorful fish in a colorful environment. It's quite a fashion icon! (84)

Trunkfish
Automobile designers at Mercedes have reconstructed a model of this fish just so they can study its streamlining. The animal's cubic shape gives it exceptional aerodynamic properties, ideal for the design and manufacture of a small car. (87)

Harlequin Sweetlip
What a change of clothes! When very small, these fish are beige with large white spots and brown rims. As they grow, their coloring is then reversed between the background and the spots.

Blue-Ringed Angelfish
This fish is so narrow that it can easily sneak between the arms and tentacles of corals and most marine life. (84)

Opah
This fish inhabits every sea, and it delights in eating jellyfish and squid. An excellent swimmer, it's able to dive into deeper waters without losing its speed. (84)

Blue-Spotted Triggerfish
This triggerfish has very thick scales that are almost welded together, thus giving it an armored protection. (87)

Pajama Cardinalfish
What an amazing dad! When the female lays her eggs, the male pajama cardinalfish scoops them up in his mouth. He then goes without eating and retains them in his mouth for up to 25 days. When they hatch, they pass quietly from out of his mouth. (85)

Leafy Sea Dragon
This really does look like a miniature dragon with leaves on it. It's not foliage, however, that's stuck to its body, but pieces of skin that enable it to camouflage itself quite well in the algae. (87)

Oranda
This is a member of the large goldfish family. It hails from China and is mostly found in aquariums, waving its long, fringed tail about like a sail. (87)

Mudskipper
This little fish inhabits mangroves. It is also given the name goby jumper, because it can get out of water and move about on land thanks to its strong, leg-like fins. Oddly enough, it would drown if it stayed under water too long! (87)

Lamprey
This species has no jaw, only little teeth. It clamps onto its prey with its mouth and uses a suction cup to dig into the flesh. This is why it is known as the vampire fish… (86)

Barracuda
With its sharp teeth, this fish is more impressive than nasty. However, if you're thinking you might try a barracuda for lunch, think again! The toxins in its flesh can lead to serious poisoning if eaten. (86)

Siamese Fighting Fish
As the name suggests, this sea creature is extremely feisty. In earlier days, it was used by organized betting circles in fish fighting contests. Today, however, it's mostly an aquarium fish to be admired for its beauty. (86/87)

Oarfish
Legend has it that this is the original serpent of the seas. Its dorsal fin practically makes up its entire body – a dozen meters (40 feet) long. It's no wonder we sometimes mistake it for a snake. (86)

Sturgeon

The mention of sturgeon evokes thoughts of caviar, the refined dish captured from the fish's eggs. As a result, though, this animal has become one of the most endangered species in Europe. (86)

Moray Eel

Watch out for the moray, as it's a voracious character. It has two rows of teeth, which allow for zero fish passing through its jaws. (87)

Thresher Shark

This shark's tail is very long, almost as long as its whole body. It uses the tail as a club to knock out any sardines in its wake – as they are its favorite food! (87)

Banded Pipefish

This fish looks like a long, striped pipe. There's a mouth on one side and on the other a red tail shaped like a small paddle. (86/87)

Ocean Sunfish

This massive creature looks like a fish without a tail. Furthermore, it is very heavy, sometimes weighing in at over a ton. (86)

Indo-Pacific Sailfish

The tail of this fish has amazing thrust power. It's without doubt the fastest fish at 100 kilometers (62 miles) per hour – just as fast as a cheetah! (86)

Pumpkinseed

This freshwater fish may be beautiful, but people have introduced it into waters where it doesn't belong. It's now often considered an invasive species. (86)

Flying Fish

This fish springs out of the water and, using its pectoral fins, appears to hover just like a seahorse. (86)

Seahorse

With its pointed head and elegant neck, this sea creature truly looks like a miniature horse without legs. It also offers a great example to all stay-at-home fathers! When the female has laid her eggs, she puts them into the ventral pocket of the male, leaving him to incubate the young. (86)

Haloed Torpedo Ray

As its name suggests, the fins on this ray send electric shocks. Medical doctors use this kind of electricity as a treatment for epilepsy. (88)

Ornate Eagle Ray

This ray is easily recognized by its projected head, large eyes and diamond shape. When it swims, it uses its large, wing-like fins to scrape the sandy bottom of the ocean floor. Such activity helps dredge up small animals that other bottom-dwelling fish eat. (88/89)

Common Skate

Have you ever discovered small, black objects on the seashore that look like pouches. They may be the dried up egg cases of skate fish. English people describe these objects as mermaid's purses. (88)

Manta Ray

It's the so-called 'devil of the seas'! In a Polynesian legend, the manta ray envelops pearl fishermen and drags them off to the bottom of the ocean. In truth, this spectacular and rather graceful creature is quite harmless to people. (88/89)